WATER
GARDENS

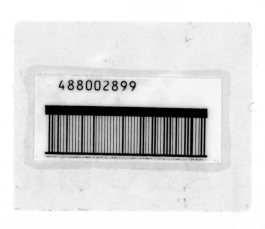

Alphabooks

A & C Black
London

Water
Gardens

Gordon T. Ledbetter

© 1989, 1979 Gordon Ledbetter

Second paperback edition 1989

Alphabooks Ltd, a subsidiary of A & C Black (Publishers) Ltd, 35 Bedford Row, London WC1R 4JH

ISBN 0-7136-3147-3

A CIP catalogue record for this book is available from the British Library.

Picture credits

The author and publisher thank the following for permission to use their photographs in this book: Chris Aldridge page 63 (top); Alphabet & Image Library 65; Heather Angel 45, 49. 50 (bottom), 57 (bottom), 106 (right), 112, 114, 116 (both), 117, 118 (bottom), 134 (top), 136 (both), 137 (top); Tony Birks-Hay 122 (bottom right); Pat Brindley 12 (both), 64, 80 (both), 84; E. Duffield 122 (bottom left); Mary Jacobsen 29; Lilypons Water Gardens 42, 66 (top), 67 (top), 67 (bottom), 70, 72 (bottom); Natural History Photographic Agency 44, 47 (top left); John Parkhurst 6, 52 (top); Roy Pearce 50 (top), 118 (top), 137 (bottom); Laurence Perkins 110; P. Scully 69; Dr. E. Sides 131; Harry Smith Horticultural Photographic Collection 16, 60, 89; Stapeley Water Gardens 122 (top); John Topham Library 2-3, 24; courtesy Louis Walsh 130; Michael Warren 35. The remaining photographs are by the author. All line drawings are by Elizabeth Winson and Peter Haillay. The author would like to thank in particular Charles Thomas of Lilypons Water Gardens, Maryland, for his interest and help in preparing the revised edition of this book.

Printed and bound by Butler & Tanner Ltd, Frome, Somerset, England

CONTENTS

The sunken, paved pond at Great Dixter, Sussex, England. The paving is York stone. The change of levels is an interesting feature in itself and adds much to the sense of unity in the garden. The grass surround and the judicious use of planting materials provide a perfect counterbalance to the hard surface. This is an outstanding example of what a patio pond should be: spacious yet intimate; mellow with plants without the planting appearing at all cramped.

1 MAKING A GARDEN POND

A music critic once remarked of one of the great sopranos of long ago (Amelita Galli-Curci), that her voice always reminded him of 'water lilies floating on water'. What the critic had in mind, of course, was an effortless, unblemished beauty, serene and chaste. It is what has made sopranos and water-lilies revered down the ages.

Water lilies, however, differ from most *prima donnas* in one important respect. They do not require cossetting, are by no means temperamental. In fact, water lilies are extremely easy to grow, as are many water-loving plants. And for the newcomer to gardening, a garden pool probably offers more certain and more rapid results than any other form of gardening. Once the initial work is completed, a pond involves less maintenance than, say, the equivalent area in grass, and much less work than a herbaceous border. Moreover, a pond can occupy a tiny space where a herbaceous border would look out of place or awkward. On the other hand, a pond can be made the centrepiece of the most ambitious combination of rockery and stone and brickwork. No other form of gardening has such wide appeal. No child can resist rushing to the pond's edge to watch the fish and glimpse the creepy crawlies. There can be few adults, even those normally indifferent to garden plants, who will not respond to the beauty of the water lily. And even the non-gardener is likely to find afternoon tea or an aperitif, taken by the pond, somehow tastes different. There is perhaps only one drawback to a water garden; and that, to be sure, is a serious one. It is simply not true that it takes half a metre of water to make a hazard for a small child. Even a puddle is a potential danger to any child who cannot swim, and that fact should never be forgotten. But that said, probably no other kind of garden is more likely to appeal to all your family; to become, indeed, a family institution.

Tub ponds

A taste for water gardening need not be an expensive one. Long gone are the days when a wealthy landowner would take it into his head to install a pond of solid lead; but one of the oldest forms of containers is still among the cheapest. Half a wooden wine barrel will make an excellent tub pond. Standing on a patio about waist high, a tub pond makes an attractive ornament in its own right. Sunk in the ground, the pressure of water within and that of the earth without will keep the wooden staves of the barrel holding water long after the metal rims have rusted away. A sunken pond is not as susceptible to changes in air temperature as a raised one, a feature for which water lilies tend to be grateful. And there are miniature water lilies which are well

7

suited to the small surface area contained in a barrel. The limited growth of these plants means that their leaves will not flop helplessly over the sides. An old china sink would do as well as a barrel — indeed any container which is at least 30 cm. deep and which holds water will serve as a tub pond.

Prefabricated ponds

Next in convenience, though a great deal more expensive, is the modern prefabricated fibreglass or plastic pond. These are usually designed with ledges upon which can be placed pots to contain marginal plants. Digging out the site to conform to the irregular shapes of most prefab ponds requires a little more skill and care than does a perfectly round barrel or a rectangular pond. Dig out the site as closely as possible to the shape of the pond, at the same time removing any sharp stones. If you leave any hollows or spaces under the pre-formed pool, being inflexible, it may be liable to crack should you stand on the base. When you are satisfied that the excavation conforms to the contours of the pond, give the base and sides of the excavation a light covering of sand. Upon this the prefabricated pond is bedded down and it is then immediately

A tub pond. Support the pots containing the marginal plants with bricks.

ready for filling. A disadvantage of prefab pools lies in their limited size; and more than that, the fact that you cannot choose or design the shape yourself which is surely half the fun.

Pool liners

By far the majority of domestic ponds are now made with flexible membranes, or liners as they are usually called. As science continually makes available new materials and refines older kinds, the range of pond liners is being expanded and improved. Generally speaking you get what you pay for; the more expensive liners are the more durable. They are also, incidentally, cheaper, metre for square metre, than pre-formed pools.

Liners are often sold under brand names, but the materials from which they are made fall into three broad categories: plastic, PVC and synthetic rubber. First the plastic liners: polyethylene (more usually called polythene) is a kind of plastic, and probably the cheapest form of pond liner going. Polythene comes in

An informal, plastic moulded pond complete with three ledges suitable for marginals.

many grades, the heavier the better. A quite different material, though sometimes confused with plastic, is PVC (polyvinyl chloride), which is available plain or with a strengthening laminate of nylon weave. Synthetic rubber such as butyl rubber, first used by the construction industry to line an irrigation canal in Utah and still in use, is widely used in Europe as a tanking material. At the moment butyl rubber is less easy to obtain in the United States, although this situation is likely to change in the near future. Butyl is a constituent polymer of another flexible rubber called EPDM (Ethylene diane polypropylene monomer) which is sometimes called butyl rubber, and indeed the two materials are virtually indistinguishable by eye. However, EPDM is manufactured to varying specifications and cheaper grades of EPDM can be toxic to fish. So, when buying a liner, go to a reputable nursery or manufacturer, who can assure you that his product is suitable for ponds, and not only as a roofing material for which some membranes are primarily used. Typical thicknesses of liners are 0.75 mm., 1 mm. and 1.5 mm. The thinnest grade, 0.75 mm., can be used successfully if economy is a priority and provided the liner is treated with care, but there is no doubt that the tiny bit of extra thickness provided by 1 mm. sheeting makes it far less susceptible to damage. This thickness is well suited to general pond applications.

The fact that all pond liners are flexible means that they will fit virtually any shape. Too many abrupt contours and narrow inlets should, nevertheless, be avoided as it means overlapping the liner rather excessively. Besides, too many nooks and crannies and small bays make a pond look fussy. Go for broad, sinuous curves if you are making an informal, natural pond. PVC, butyl rubber and EPDM have the advantage of being stretchable as well as flexible. But I would not attempt to stretch-fit an elastic liner; in fact I make a

Begin your pond by mapping out the circumference with a length of rope. View the result from every conceivable angle; make sure you have sufficient room all round the pond and make any necessary adjustments. Use an edge cutter and a spade to cut and lift the turves.

point of laying all liners on the loose side. Even though it means a certain number of wrinkles may remain, they will not be noticeable once the pond is complete. If the membrane is ever punctured when it is taut and under tension, the hole will open and may even run. Remember, too, that once the pond is filled, the weight of water may compress the banks and base, making the liner that much tighter than you intended. Ideally the liner should not be secured around the top of the pond until after the pond has been filled. When that is impractical, or you want to complete the job in one go, leave a little additional slack.

Before cutting a single sod, map out the circumference of the pond you have in mind using a length of rope. (You might begin by putting your plan down on paper.) Remove the grass sods or the first few centimetres of soil within the area of the rope and you then have a blueprint of your pond. Any final modifications should be carried out at this stage. There is no difficulty about cutting out additional space in the pond later. But banking-up crumbling soil to fill an unwanted corner

Once you have excavated the site, make sure that the banks are level all round. This is a tedious job but one worth taking time over. Incidentally, if you want to test that your level is in working order, place it on a straight piece of wood as in the picture to obtain a level reading. Then reverse it and if the bubble stays between the two marks then your level is giving correct readings. The shelf running the length of the left-hand bank and the bank at the far end will be used later to support marginal plants grown in baskets.

With the site fully prepared, the liner can be unfolded. In this case it is a PVC liner. If the day is warm, there is no harm in allowing the fully opened liner to lie in the sun for a few hours. This will add to its flexibility.

BELOW *Lay the liner across the site and keep in place with bricks. You will find this job much easier to carry out if you choose a calm day.*

or to make a promontory is much more trouble than leaving firm, well-packed soil where it stands. The same applies to ledges. When digging out the site, where you want ledges leave 30 cm. or more of bank between the rope and the excavation. Then remove soil from the bank to a depth of about 25 to 30 cm., that is to say the depth of the planting pot you intend using, plus a few centimetres so the pot will be completely concealed under water. Allowance should also be made for the fact that the water level will normally be a little below the top of the liner. (Even if you fill the pond to the very brim, the lapping effect of water will reduce the level slightly.) Finally, all sharp or flinty stones must be scrupulously removed from the site before installing the liner. By adding a few centimetres of sand — easily applied when damp — to the base and sides, it will be possible to stand in the finished pool without fear of damaging it — provided you wear soft-soled shoes. As an alternative to sand, polyester matting is available in rolls and when laid out and overlapped will provide a protective base for your liner; it can be used for the sides too, of course. It is simpler and cleaner to bring a roll of polyester through the house than to cart through sand when there is no other access to the garden. Matting is also quicker to lay than sand, though if the bottom of the excavation is very rough, with the points of large stones that cannot be readily removed showing through, a thick layer of sand offers the best protection for your liner.

Small fountain ornaments, if their bases are quite smooth, can be stood on liners quite safely. In the case of heavy ornaments, such as cast-iron fountains or big statues, which might make a depression in the ground and become lop-sided in the process, it is advisable to put in a footing of concrete, say 5–10 cm., beneath the liner. (The concrete should be composed of cement, sand and coarse aggregate in the ratio 1:2:3 or 1:2:4.) Make the footing a little wider and broader than the base of the ornament, smooth the top edges of the footing, and make sure the footing is flush with the surrounding ground. The ground beneath the footing should be well compacted. Cover the concrete with a piece of polyester matting before laying the liner. The ornament itself can be placed on the liner, with a spare piece of matting or corner cut off the liner sandwiched between; or another thickness of concrete can be added inside the liner, if it is necessary to raise the ornament.

So much for the preparation of the site. To calculate the size of the liner for your pond, add twice the depth to the length and multiply by twice the depth added to the width. For example, if your excavation measures 2.4 by 1.9 by 0.5 metres deep, the dimensions of the sheet of liner will be 2.4 + 1 by 1.9 + 1, which works out as 3.4 metres long and 2.9 metres wide. To these dimensions you should add about 60 cm. to both the length and the width, to allow the liner to overlap the top of the banks where it can be secured. So the final dimensions for the pond in question would be 4.0 × 3.5 metres, which is to say the sheet will be exactly 14 square metres. If your pond has any ledges along its length or width, you must take these into account as the surface area of the excavation will be greater than if the pond had only gently sloping sides. In this case, simply drape a builder's tape the length of the pond, starting at the top of one bank, across the base and up the bank at the far side. Do the same across the width.

A flexible liner can be installed in one of two ways. With very small ponds the liner can be laid across the excavation with bricks holding it around the sides, then direct a hose pipe into the centre of the pool and watch the weight of water smooth the liner over the base, making it cling to the sides with a minimum of wrinkling. You can assist the process by alternately releasing the liner from under some bricks, pulling it up further under others as necessary.

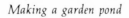

Making a garden pond

Removing stones from the site and making a marginal shelf.
BELOW *A liner is held in place with planks; the rising water forces it against the sides of the site.*

This method is hardly practical for large ponds, so the liner should be laid on the base and smoothed against the sides by hand, making absolutely certain that no hollows are left between liner and bank. Where the pond has deep bays and broad promontories you may find that a certain amount of overlapping and wrinkles is inevitable. If you wish, these overlaps can be glued down to provide a smoother finish, but the weight of water will tend to flatten such overlaps, and, in any case, you will not notice wrinkles once the pond is established.

In formal ponds, if a liner in sheet form is used to make a strictly rectangular pond, for example, you will have no choice but neatly to pleat the corners and glue the pleats back against the walls. A better finish is achieved by using a liner made up in boxed or three-dimensional form. Many specialist suppliers, especially of butyl rubber, will weld liners into any formal shape. All that is then necessary is to slot the liner into the excavation in question. Needless to say, the measurements you give the supplier must be accurate. It is best to prepare the excavation first, as there may be a small but significant variation between planned and actual dimensions.

Formal ponds are generally made with vertical sides. This may not be possible to achieve with sub soil which tends to crumble when cut vertically; and a point worth remembering is that vertical banks can collapse inwards after heavy rain, especially if the pond is standing empty. So formal ponds with vertical sides are often first lined with block or brick prior to the installation of a flexible membrane, a considerable addition to costs.

The flexible liner may be secured at the top of the bank under paving slabs, bricks, crazy paving etc., bedded down on mortar (sand and cement in the ratio of 3:1). Remember that lime, which is toxic to fish, may leech out of the mortar into the pond, necessitating several changes of water before first plants and then

When cementing the surround in place — in this instance bricks are being used — try to keep the liner taut as you lay the cement. Use a level when laying the bricks.

fish — always in that order — are introduced.

If your pond is sited on a lawn you may prefer to have grass meeting the water's edge rather than slabs or bricks. In this case cut grass turves in even rectangular lengths, sufficient for the perimeter of the pond, before excavating the site. Try to cut the turves to equal thickness. The liner can be tucked into a narrow slit trench at a convenient distance from the edge and the turves then laid over the liner. The trench, however, is optional. If you lay the turves after the pond has been filled there is no reason why the liner should slip from under the turves, and once the roots of the grass knit together the liner becomes immovable. Sometimes, if the lawn becomes very dry, a yellow rim of even drier grass may become apparent around the pond, because the liner is preventing the grass immediately above it from drawing moisture from the ground beneath. For this reason keep the overlap of liner to a minimum.

A few centimetres of liner showing above water level is ugly. It is also an obvious giveaway if you are trying to make the pond look natural. There is a solution. Lay one or more courses of brick or stone or a material suited to your design on a ledge beneath the final coping, with the liner concealed behind it (see drawing). The improvement this kind of work can make to your pond can hardly be overstated.

There is much to be said for having a permanent means of keeping the pond topped up in preference to the chore of having to connect up a hose pipe and drag it half way round the garden. A water pipe can be concealed in the depths of the pond, brought through the bank or over the top concealed among rocks. If it is used in connection with an electrical probe and solenoid valve, it will keep your pond at a precise level all the time. The electrical probe is fixed in the pond at the appropriate level, and should be arranged so that fine adjustment is possible. It is wired up via a transformer to the solenoid valve, which is spring-loaded to remain permanently closed unless electrically activated. The valve is connected in line with the water pipe at any convenient point, and requires weatherproof protection. The installation of this kind of equipment should be carried out by a qualified electrician.

Pipework

If you live in an area of high rainfall and your garden has poor drainage, it may be necessary

A liner can be protected from ultra-violet rays (and mechanical damage) by a perimeter line of rocks or bricks, as shown.

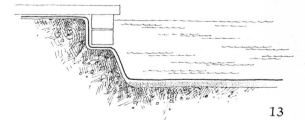

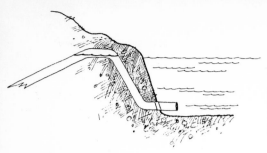

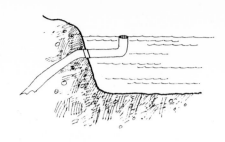

Two ways of arranging an overflow pipe. Each method has advantages and disadvantages. Use the one best suited to your situation (see text).

to have an overflow pipe to avoid flooding around your pond. This can be arranged in one of two ways (see drawings). The advantage of the overflow pipe opening vertically at water level, is that the whole cross section of the pipe will take water once the water level rises. As against that, a pipe breaking the surface may be conspicuous and leaves and debris tend to collect around it. A mesh cover is essential and will require periodic cleaning. The second method is much more discreet, less likely to lead to clogging, and should be maintenance free. However, it does require higher ground somewhere around the pond in order to conceal the pipe. It also means that if the pipe is arranged so that it takes no water until *after* the pond is completely full (obviously the most attractive level to have the pond), then the overflow will not become fully operative until the water level has risen virtually, or in fact, to flood point. Clearly this arrangement is most appropriate in a pond surrounded by sloping lawns, where the ground close to the pond can absorb a limited amount of water over a brief period.

PVC pipes can be brought through liners by means of flanges (see drawings). Small-bore pipes need only screw-type flanges, the washers being liberally coated with mastic before being pressed together. Large pipes require flanges that are bolted together, mastic being applied to the bolt holes, which are not otherwise waterproof. You will have to punch out a hole not only for the pipe, but also for each of the bolts, an easy enough job in theory, but in practice one which requires care. If the bolt holes are not exactly positioned you may end up with wrinkles in the liner that are hard to smooth out; and, of

course, if the liner is crimped instead of lying flat between the flanges you may not get a waterproof joint. An alternative is to use a flange made up of the flexible material you are using for the pond lining. Again specialist suppliers can provide you with a flange and sleeve made up to the appropriate size. Work the pipe through the sleeve before you attempt to attach the flange. All that is then required is to apply glue to both surfaces, or cold tape (as opposed to vulcanising tape which has to be heated) as an alternative in the case of butyl and EPDM, and then smooth the flange against the liner, using a piece of timber as a temporary backing support. It is very important to keep the liner as flat and wrinkle-free as possible when you bring the flange to it. Mastic can then be applied the whole way round the flange. The sleeve can be rolled back a few centimetres and glue applied to the pipe before rolling the sleeve back again. Mastic can be applied to the end of the sleeve, or you can use a jubilee clip for an extra strong joint with the pipe.

Flanges make it possible to bring a pipe through the side of a pond without the problem of causing a leak. For thin membranes such as butyl and EPDM, you can use (a) a flexible flange and sleeve made of the same material as the liner; (b) a rigid PVC flange with bolts; or (c) a PVC screw-type flange.

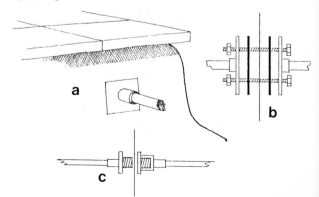

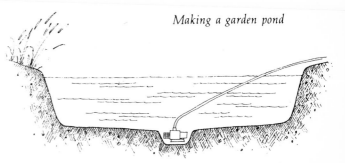

To empty your pond with a temporary submersible pump, make sure the pond has a sump towards which the base slopes gently.

Old text books on pond construction nearly all suggested that you should put a pipe into the bottom of the pond for drainage purposes, and there would be a neat diagram showing the pipe leading off into a French drain. What the books rarely said was how much additional work there is in digging a trench for an outlet pipe. For Koi ponds, an outlet pipe can be of special importance as a means of removing detritus and mulm from the pond (see Chapter 8). To drain an ordinary pond it is much simpler to use a portable electric submersible pump occasionally, than to incorporate an outlet pipe. Just remember to dig a sump for the pump when making your pond and have the base sloping towards it (see drawing).

Choice of liner

So which kind of pond liner should you go for? Pond liners can suffer from two kinds of damage: puncturing (more rarely tearing), and the effects of ultra-violet light. The area of the liner above water level, if constantly exposed to the sun, is the vulnerable area. Plastics break down most quickly in the presence of ultra-violet light, the tell-tale symptoms being the liner becoming brittle and then cracking. Polythene is easily punctured and very susceptible to the sun, black polythene less so; certain other plastics formulated to withstand ultra-violet rays offer greater longevity, such as *Trocal T.8*. PVC is a durable material, while butyl rubber and EPDM are generally regarded as the most durable and toughest of all. Garden centres stock liners in a variety of standard sizes. Fabrication of butyl sheeting and EPDM is possible up to 1000 square metres, after which it becomes too heavy and unwieldy to lay as a single sheet and should be jointed on site. Butyl weighs about 1.20 kg. per square metre, so there is over one tonne in 1000 square metres. If you are laying a large sheet and need to adjust its position, get several pairs of hands to flap air under the liner and then pull it towards you, repeating the operation as necessary. Otherwise, butyl lying on sand forms an effective vacuum and will hardly shift. Avoid brightly coloured liners; whatever manufacturers may say about their product being algae resistant, it can only be a question of degree. Algae will adhere to all surfaces, and on other than black or very dark colours will quickly show up.

Repairs are possible to all these materials: polythene can be repaired with adhesive tape, or heat welded (a specialised skill); certain plastics and PVC can be repaired with solvent glues; butyl rubber and EPDM by vulcanising (which requires a special heating press — like a trouser press — that is usually only available to the fabricator of the material), or by rubber tape or glue and the repair patch sealed with mastic. A point to be noted is that most home-repairs are permanent only if the area surrounding the puncture or tear is not under tension, which is another reason for avoiding stretch-fitting of your liner. With that proviso, it can be said that a top quality liner properly installed and treated with reasonable care will last indefinitely.

Concrete

Flexible liners have largely replaced concrete for making garden ponds. But concrete retains one great advantage: it cannot be punctured, though of course it can crack. It is possible to have the best of both worlds by having a flexible membrane overlaid with concrete. Let this concrete develop hair cracks — it does not have to be waterproof nor as thick as a pond made wholly of concrete, its function is simply to protect the liner. There is no question but that such a combination of materials adds greatly to the cost, not to mention the additional work involved. If you are caring for your pond yourself and carrying out the maintenance, you might not think a 'double skin' worthwhile, but I have used this method in public parks and the like where it is hard to know what sort of treatment the ponds may get over the years.

All that is required is to overlay all internal surfaces, the base and sides, with about 8 cm. of concrete (the mix being cement, sand and coarse aggregate in the ratio 1:2:4; or use ready-mix for convenience). It is vitally important that the membrane is perfectly waterproof and free of holes before starting, and that none is made while laying the concrete, otherwise it will be all but impossible to locate a leak after the concrete has been laid. The base can be concreted with or without reinforcement (you are not overly concerned with cracks), but the sides do need mesh, and chicken-wire with *wide* holes does very well. Liners have shiny surfaces and if you try to get concrete to stay up on the sides, even if they are sloping, the concrete will slide off. So make up a bucket of pure cement with water — a soupy mix will do very well — and apply to the sides with a brush. Let the cement dry, and you will find that the concrete will adhere to the sides and, with aid of the chicken-wire, stay in place. The chicken-wire can be bedded into the base to make a good joint for the concrete. Smooth off the concrete and the job is done. Formal ponds with vertical sides will require shuttering.

The roots of plants or trees are rarely a problem with flexible, elastic membranes, but what if there is a need to plant or dig up

A fine example of a concrete pool. Note how the paving elements slightly overhang the bank.

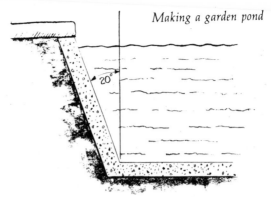

shrubs close to your pond? It requires great care not to damage a liner when wielding a spade or fork.

A concrete pond can certainly be very durable, but only if built to the highest standards in the first place. Compromise on the preparation of the site or in the thickness of the concrete, omit reinforcement in the concrete, fail to allow for the expansion of water into ice, and disaster may well follow.

To begin with, satisfy yourself that the site is firm and stable. If in doubt thoroughly bed into the base and sides a layer of coarse aggregate (gravel). In an informal pond the sides should be cut so as to slope outwards at an angle of 20° or more off the perpendicular. This will reduce the pressure exerted on the concrete when ice forms, as the ice will tend to rise upwards as it expands. If the sides have to be perfectly vertical, as is usual with formal schemes, then the sides should be made as thick as the base. That is to say not less than 15 cm. thick. Sloping walls need to be at least 12 cm. thick, and it is important to avoid one very common mistake: do not allow the cement to slide down and bulge at the bottom of the wall so that it is thinner at the top. The concrete should be mixed in the proportions: one part of cement by volume to two of sand and three of aggregate. The aggregate should be composed of either gravel or crushed stone varying in size between 5 mm. and 20 mm. Use only materials supplied by a building merchant; should the sand or gravel contain any organic matter, such as decaying leaves, the strength of the concrete will be impaired and may even become porous. The addition of a waterproofing agent will improve the impermeability and durability of the concrete, although it is not a cure for concrete that is improperly mixed or sub-standard for any reason. Do mix the materials *dry*, and mix them all thoroughly.

Then, and only then, add water. Failure to observe this procedure may result in the

The walls of concrete ponds are far less vulnerable to the pressure of ice if they are not perfectly upright. Aim for a slope of about 20° off the perpendicular.

materials never being properly mixed. Add no more water than is necessary to obtain a consistency whereby it is possible to slice the concrete with a spade without the two sides becoming completely united again. Standard reinforcing steel mesh or heavy gauge chicken-wire — and steel rods if it is a really large pond — should be used to reinforce the concrete. Care must be taken to ensure that the concrete penetrates the spaces between the wire meshes without leaving innumerable air spaces like a sponge. Rust is no problem, but wire which for any reason has been painted is unsuitable, and leaves or grass which have become enmeshed in chicken-wire must be thoroughly removed, or the wire rejected.

The life of concrete can be considerably extended by removing the air spaces that naturally form during mixing and laying. Use a vibrating poker vertically or along its side, dipping the poker into the wet concrete at close intervals. This helps the air spaces and miniscule honeycombs to collapse and the air to escape. Vibrator pokers can be readily hired.

Formal ponds with perpendicular sides will need what is known as 'shuttering' to keep the concrete in place while it hardens. Shuttering consists of a frame (with easily removable sides) made of wood, chipboard or even hardboard and designed to fit into the pit leaving a gap the whole way round of 15 cm. Soapy water lathered on to the bank side of the shuttering will help to prevent the wood adhering to the concrete.

Concrete begins setting immediately it becomes wet. It stiffens noticeably after about twenty minutes in warm weather, and more rapidly in hot. The process can be slowed down by continually turning the mix over. It is as well to dampen the interior of the site. This will prevent the concrete losing moisture too rapidly once it is in place, which would have the effect of reducing its ultimate strength. Begin by laying down about 6 cm. of concrete over the base. Place the reinforcement over this and then add concrete to make up the final thickness of 15 cm. Make sure that the wire mesh is completely smothered in the concrete without protruding at any point, except around the banks where it will be used to reinforce the sides. In the case of an informal pond, it should be possible to concrete the base and sides in one single operation. With small, formal ponds you may be able to put the shuttering in place while the base is still soft and so proceed immediately with the sides. (It really depends upon the weight of the shuttering and whether it can be installed without the necessity of walking on the base.) If you cannot put the shuttering in straight away, key or roughen the edges of the base to make a good joint with the sides later. Allow the base to harden, install the shuttering and add the walls. Old concrete will not bond with new, so the sooner the walls are added the better — I would certainly not leave the adding of the walls for weeks on end. Also, the earth banks will tend to crumble to some extent and it is imperative that you do not get soil mixed with the concrete at any stage. The fact, incidentally, that you have dampened the walls should help. Lining the excavation with cheap polythene may be necessary if the sub-soil is very crumbly. If the weather is very hot it is as well to lay wet sacks over the concrete while it hardens. The more slowly it loses moisture the better the concrete. Indeed it is worth filling the pond with water after twenty-four hours.

Calculate the amount of concrete you need by adding the surface area of the four walls to the area of the base and multiplying that figure by the thickness you intend making the concrete. For example, if you were making a pond 5 m. x 4 m. x 0.9 m. internal depth with the base and walls 15cm. thick, the calculations would be made as follows:

$$2 (5 \times 0.9) = 9 \text{ sq. metres}$$
(the two longer walls)

$$2 (3.7 \times 0.9) = 6.66 \text{ sq. metres}$$
(the two shorter walls)
i.e. each length less 2 x 0.15 cm. which is the thickness of the longer walls

$$5 \times 4 = 20 \text{ sq. metres} \quad \text{(the base)}$$

The total surface area therefore amounts to approximately 36 sq. metres. Multiply by the thickness: $36 \times 0.15 = 5.4$ cubic metres, which is the amount of concrete the pond requires. Ready-mixed concrete becomes economical for any size of load above 3 cubic metres. One would be well advised to have so large a load as 5.4 cubic metres supplied ready-mixed by lorry, provided, of course, that the lorry can approach the site. Failing that, look into the possibility of hiring a small, portable cement mixer. In this case add half the coarse aggregate and half the water first, then add the sand. Once they are mixed, add the cement and finally the remainder of the coarse aggregate and enough water to produce the necessary consistency. The materials should be carefully measured by volume, using a bucket, for example.

If you are buying the materials to mix yourself, then they should be calculated as follows. The ratio of the mix is 1 cement : 2 sand :

Making a garden pond

RIGHT *Shuttering for a formal pond. It must be rigid but easily dismantled.*

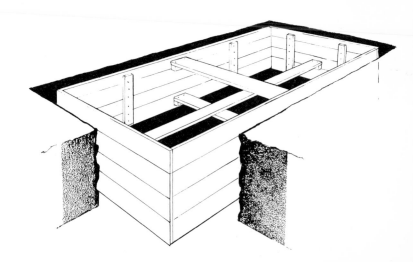

BELOW *The well-defined border of this rectangular pond helps to define the area of water from the surrounding grass. Without so strong a border the pond would be far less conspicuous.*

3 aggregate, that is to say there are 6 parts to the whole. Therefore, in 5.4 cubic metres one part will consist of $5.4 \div 6 = 0.9$ cubic metres. So one needs:

> 0.9 cubic metres of cement
> 1.8 cubic metres of sand
> 2.7 cubic metres of coarse aggregate

You may find that the builder's merchant supplies the materials not according to cubic capacity but according to weight. Unfortunately, there is no fixed ratio between the weight and cubic capacity of either sand or coarse aggregate. The ratio varies according to the character of the materials. It is better to use the density of concrete as a unit of measurement. (This is not absolutely accurate, but it is quite sufficient for pond building.) The density of concrete can be set at 2.45 metric tonnes per cubic metre. So for 5.4 cubic metres the weight would be 13.23 metric tonnes. The materials can now be calculated as follows:

CEMENT: $\dfrac{13.23}{6} = 2.205$ tonnes

Each bag of cement weighs 50 kilos, so 45 (44.1) bags are required.

SAND: $\dfrac{13.23}{6} \times 2 = 4.41$ (say 5 tonnes)

AGGREGATE: $\dfrac{13.23}{6} \times 3 = 6.615$ (say 7 tonnes)

It is always safer to slightly overestimate your needs to allow for wastage. Remember that the number of joints should be kept to a minimum. Try to complete the pond in no more than two operations.

If you live in an area with very severe winters, you can make a concrete pond of great strength by employing a technique more usually used for swimming pools. It consists of building a double wall of concrete blocks and filling the gap between the two walls with solid concrete. Steel rods can be inserted in the blocks as they are laid and this will provide massive strength. The blocks will not be waterproof, they simply provide the strength. It is the concrete between the two walls that makes the pond watertight and it must be very thoroughly compacted. An important point to note is that when laying the blocks, surplus mortar must not be allowed to collect on the base between the two walls. If it does, the inner concrete wall may not make a watertight joint with the base.

This is an expensive method of pond building and a time-consuming one. As against that, it does mean shuttering is avoided and this is worth bearing in mind where large-scale, geometric designs are concerned.

Whereas with fibreglass and liner ponds it is usually possible to make some adjustment to the level of the walls after the pond is completed, with concrete structures it is much more difficult to do and achieve a watertight bond. You may find you have to use a sealant compound, or rapid hardening cement (which is applied like a paste), to get a waterproof joint. Nothing looks worse than water halfway up one bank and brimming over the other. So it is worth taking the trouble to level the site before carrying out the concreting. Use a straight board and a level. If the site is too large to stretch the board from one bank to the other, drive a stake into the centre of the base so that it is level with the lowest bank. Then remove the surplus soil from the other banks, taking readings with the board and level as you go. What is known as a line level, this is to say a level that can be suspended from a horizontal cord or string (see drawing), can provide accurate results too. The greatest accuracy is achieved with a dumpy level and staff. You set the level (which is like a telescope) up on a tripod, level it, and read off the markings on the staff while it is perched at various points around the top of the pond. If point A reads 1.2 metres and point B 1.35 metres, then you know that B with the *higher* reading is in fact *lower* than A, by 15 cm. in fact (1.35-1.2). Hire a dumpy level for a day or two if your pond is a large one. What will *not* provide accurate levels is to go round the perimeter of the pond taking one level off the next with a builder's level. One small error is compounded by the next and by the time you have gone the whole way round, you will be 'out' by quite a bit. What you should do with all methods of levelling is to use one datum point against which all other points are compared.

Concrete is best suited to small ponds of comparatively uniform width and length. When you have a design in which the pond quickly narrows and broadens again, you are liable to set up stress points. Similarly stress is likely to occur if the length of the pond is appreciably more than its width. A concrete pond that is larger than, say, 4.5 × 4.5 metres is likely to require laying sections with what are known as water bars between them, and this takes the concrete pond into the area of engineering.

Flanged pipes can be embedded successfully in concrete — there are flanges specially made for the purpose — and mastic is applied round where the pipe meets the concrete face, as a precautionary measure.

Alkali will leach out the water from the new concrete, and this is harmful to both plants and fish. It can be prevented by painting the interior surfaces of the new pond with a

sealing agent. Alternatively, the new pond can be seasoned by filling and emptying it of water several times over a period of some weeks. Acetic acid or 'Glacial acetic acid', otherwise known as vinegar, if applied to the concrete with a paintbrush can speed up the seasoning process, but of course the acid must be washed out of the pond after use.

Concrete can be repaired either with rapid hardening cement or a proprietary sealant, spread over the crack and beyond it for a fair distance — at least 15 cm. The area should first be treated with an anti-algicide or fungicide, if the pond is an old one, or given a good rubbing-over with a wire brush. If the concrete is actually broken into pieces as opposed to being simply cracked, then the loose bits should be removed and fresh concrete used to fill the cavities.

Renderings

There is one further method of making a pond or restoring an old one that is worth considering. There are on the market a number of materials which can be applied rather in the manner of paint to a hard surface such as *in situ* concrete and block walls. *Poolcrete* is one such preparation; another is *Elastoflex* which is described as 'elastic concrete'. It is a polymer which is mixed with cement and sand (the proportions to vary according to whether the material is to be used as a grout or a rendering). When cured it is the colour of khaki, and is rather like a rubbery linoleum. The advantage of such a flexible material is that it can take movement in the supporting wall in the way that a mortar rendering cannot.

For intricate geometric pond designs, construction by block and rendering offers a very precise finish that would be more difficult to achieve with block and flexible sheeting, even in three-dimensional form, for some element of slack is likely to be visible in a very formal

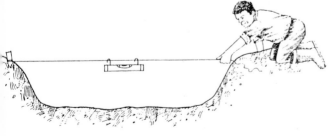

A line level, enlarged for clarity, shown in use.

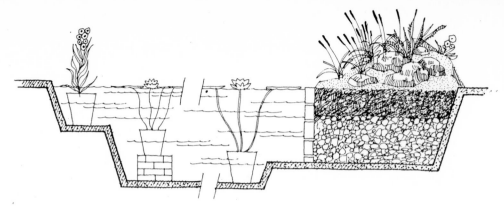

Cross-section of a pond showing how planting depths can be arranged.

design. Rendering is also economical, in that the block work is, in any case, essential to produce an intricate design with precision (see p. 29).

The problem of how to deal with an old, leaking concrete pond is one that arises quite often. To take up the concrete and re-line the pond with fresh concrete is a major undertaking. Putting new concrete over the old will make the pond smaller, and is impractical if the pond is exactly framed by an existing patio. Laying a liner over the concrete is certainly a possibility, once all rough edges and loose concrete have been dealt with. But, again, what if there are slabs around the pond? They may be difficult to prize up without damage. Here a rendering of the old concrete becomes an attractive option, for the rendering can be brought right up to the edge of the paving slab.

Finally, you are bound to have mused over how deep to make your pond. Much is sometimes made of the relationship between surface area and water depth in the control of unsightly algae. This is a little misleading in that so far as domestic ponds are concerned, the difference between 50 cm. and 1 metre is hardly significant. In deep bodies of water such as lakes, algae growth may be kept in check because of factors related to depth and light penetration, upon which algae depend.

Also, where water is deep it lies in layers according to temperature, and the intermingling and exchange between these layers inhibit algae growth. In a garden pond sunlight is likely to reach right to the bottom (except where impeded by the leaves of floating plants), and the water temperature will not be layered in quite the same way as it is in a lake.

Deep ponds are more attractive than shallow ones, but the main consideration as to how deep to make your pond is the depth of water that various water lilies like over their crowns (see Chapter 4). Generally speaking, if one allows a depth of 20–30 cm. for the soil and 25 to 75 cm. for the water above the soil, that is sufficient. In other words, a total depth of between 45 and 100 cm. Only where large water schemes are concerned, or where Koi carp are your primary interest (see Chapter 8), is it worth increasing the depth above 1 metre. If the pond has to be deeper — some ornamental ponds also serve as a source of water for fire fighting — the water lily containers can be supported on bricks at the appropriate depth.

2
DESIGNING
A POND

A good landscape designer and a good photographer have much in common. Just as a good photographer knows exactly how to compose his shot before taking it, so a good landscape designer should have a clear idea of what he wants before starting work on the site. Considerable experience is required in order to visualize precisely how any particular design may look in practice. Few amateur gardeners — and by no means all professionals — can accurately conceive a project entirely on paper or in their heads. Most gardeners will modify their initial scheme as it progresses. Nevertheless, the more clearly you can visualize and plan your water garden in advance the more satisfactory will be the result.

If design seems a daunting task, as it does to some, remember that good design is less a question of following blinding flashes of inspiration so much as satisfying some very basic, practical questions; and if you can do that there is no reason why you should not come up with a very creditable result. You should begin by asking yourself whether it is a formal or informal pond that you want. The rest of the garden may determine your choice. Have you considered having a patio with the pond? Is the site you have in mind for the pond the best position as regards sunlight and being able to see the pond from the house? And what about size? Lay out a rope to represent the perimeter of the pond, and make sure there is plenty of free space to walk around the pond. (When you start the excavation work the pit will look out of all proportion to the surroundings and you will be sure to think you have made the pond too big. However, the real consideration is the walking space around the pond. Once the excavation has been filled first with water and then plants, it is surprising how the pond shrinks.)

What are you going to do with the sub-soil removed from the site? Think of how you might embellish your pond. A fountain looks well in a formal scheme, and bear in mind that if you intend having filtration tanks (see Chapter 8) they have to be concealed somewhere.

The patio pond

If you live in an inner city environment with no more than a small but sunny patch of ground for a garden, then a patio water garden might well be the answer. A tatty patch of lawn with one or two meagre shrubs can hardly be regarded as a garden at all; but a patio and pool can, and with no more maintenance, indeed less, than that required of a lawn of the same area. Moreover, a pond, no matter how small, is a legitimate focal point in a way that a rose bush is not. If you doubt this, consider the suggestion: 'Let's have lunch round the rose bush.' Nothing sounds more odd, and nothing more natural than:

A formal Mediterranean water garden. The layout is admirable but has sufficient space been left for walking around the corners of the pond?

'Let's have lunch round the pond.' Countless thousands of backyards, too small and ugly for conventional gardening, could be transformed by making them into patio water gardens. If you are a person who is away from home for long periods, who only sees the garden at weekends, who likes neither weeding nor mowing the lawn, a patio water garden offers the ideal solution. The same is true if you happen to be the fortunate owner of a *pied-à-terre* away in the country or in some foreign land. A patio water garden can still look fresh and attractive after long periods of neglect. Finally, a patio and pond offer opportunities to anyone who owns a roof garden, which is usually limited to potted shrubs.

For the owner of a large garden, a patio pond is likely to be regarded as no more than an optional extra. No one would want to convert a whole area of rolling lawns and well laid out borders into paving stones and water. The most popular idea in such cases is to combine the patio with the back wall of the house, the pond perhaps being visible from the house through French windows (but not so close to the windows that one steps straight out of the house into the pond!). Wherever the patio is situated, so far as a large garden is concerned, it should be combined with some other feature of the garden — if not the back of the house, then a hedge or a wall (p. 35). A patio, alone, in the middle of a garden of any size will look stark and out of place.

Patio ponds are usually formal in design. A formal, regular shape nearly always harmonizes best with the strong, clear shapes of paving stones or bricks. But a pond should never be square. For some strange reason, a square always appears dull, even deadening (which presumably accounts for that piece of American slang: 'He's a square'). Make your pool rectangular; and if you have sufficient space, you might have one large rectangle bordered at each corner by a smaller one. Or

the pond might consist of two interlocking rectangles. There is no limit to the number of geometric designs one can envisage. But do not make the pond too complicated or fussy. One soon becomes irritated with a fussy design. And above all, do not make your pond so broad or long that you cannot walk the whole way round it with plenty of space to spare. Quite apart from the fact that every visitor under the age of eleven will be certain to fall into the pond or make a good attempt at doing so, you want to give the patio a sense of spaciousness. The patio should never appear to have been squeezed in, as an afterthought, between the pond and the surrounding wall. The smaller the patio, the smaller should be the pond in proportion to it. Rarely should the length and width of the pond exceed one third of the length and width of the patio.

This is even more important if you decide upon a raised pond. If your space is limited, a raised pond will tend to make the area appear even more confined. On the other hand, if

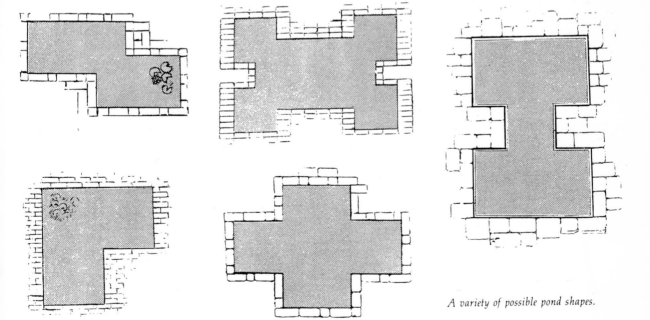

A variety of possible pond shapes.

your patio is surrounded by wrought iron work or a light railing, as is the case with many roof and terrace gardens, a raised pond will help create a welcome sense of solidity. And it does have the advantage of bringing the plants and livestock closer to view. (Having a broad coping stone on the wall makes an excellent seat.) Flexible liners can be used for raised ponds just as well as concrete. The liner simply needs to be held in place by being cemented between the last line of bricks and the coping stone.

When levelling the patio area it will also be necessary to take into account the thickness of the paving units. To do this, mark the thickness of the unit on the ends of a series of wooden pegs. Drive the pegs into the ground so that the tops are flush with the earth surrounding the patio area. The ground should then be skimmed off until the marks appear. It is very important to compact the subsoil well, otherwise settlement of your paving units will occur and you will end up with an uneven patio.

If you are using paving units which are regular in shape, then the length and width of the patio and of the pond must be multiples of the measurements of one such unit. For example, let us say that one paving slab measures 75 x 90 cm. Then the width of the pond should be a multiple of 75, and the length a multiple of 90. For example, if it were planned that two paving slabs should match the length and width of the pond, then the pond would have to measure 2 x 75 cm. by 2 x 90 cm. i.e. 1.5 x 1.8 metres. On the basis that the patio should not be less than three times as long and as wide as the pond, it must measure at least 4.5 x 5.4 metres. So for this patio 32 paving slabs are required: $(24.3 - 2.7) \div 0.675$ (i.e. the total area of the patio minus the area for the pond, divided by the area of one paving unit).

When a large number of small paving units is involved, it may be necessary to take into

An outstanding example of a formal patio pond on Roman lines, designed by H. A. Peto (1854–1933), on the island of Ilnaculin (Garinish), Co. Cork, Ireland.

Levelling a site by means of pegs and a level

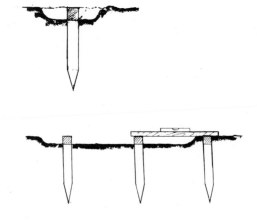

account the width of the joints, and modify the dimensions of the pond accordingly. However, this is not usually necessary with small patios as the width of the joints can be taken up by a slight overhang of the units immediately surrounding the pond. (To standardize the width of the joints, a couple of wooden pegs — about 13 mm. thick — can be placed temporarily between the units.)

There is little difficulty about using large paving slabs. But laying down a complicated pattern needs a great deal of forethought and measurements have to be exactly right. And it becomes more difficult when the paving units are of more than one kind or colour. There is a useful moral in the cartoon of the little man laying down black and white tiles in a baronial hall. He comes to the last space and then discovers that whether it be a black or white tile that he puts down, he is going to have two tiles of the same colour side by side. It is not a bad idea to lay out the pattern before excavating the pond. This way you can be certain that the dimensions of the pond fit the pattern.

Concrete slabs can be safely laid on sand, or set in mortar. The slabs round the pond, no matter how immovable they may seem, are best set in mortar. Make sure the earth is very firmly tamped down before laying the slabs, and add coarse aggregate if necessary. Small paving elements, such as cobbles, tiles and bricks should be set in mortar. It is often more satisfactory to prepare a solid concrete foundation 50-60 mm. thick, prior to bedding down the paving elements on mortar. Due allowance must be made for the depth of the paving element, the mortar and concrete

A lovely combination of water, lilies, ferns and large paving elements. Again note how the elements overhang the pond by several centimetres.

foundation. And if the patio is bordered by a lawn, sink the paving elements by an additional 15 mm. in order to facilitate cutting of the grass. The mortar can be made by mixing one part of cement with three of sand. Be sparing with the water. Spread the mortar to a thickness of about 25 mm. (50 mm. in the case of sand), lay down the paving stone and lightly tap into position. Any mortar that gets on the surface of the paving slabs should be wiped off immediately to prevent staining. The joints can be filled later with mortar or sand, depending upon which you have used for the foundation. You might find a dry-mix mortar speeds up this operation. Fill the joints with the cement and sand mix, then, very lightly, add the water. The risk of staining the patio is reduced with this method.

Irregular stone is by far the easiest kind of paving to lay. The only point to remember is that all the large pieces should not be clumped together in one part of the patio and all the smaller ones in another. This can happen if you do not start off with the firm idea of mixing all sizes together. If you want an informal pond, then 'crazy paving' or irregular stone is the obvious material to use, and will look well in almost any scheme.

ABOVE *A superb example of brickwork. The curving steps heighten the sense of the pond being the central feature.*

RIGHT *Right angles and circular forms combine to make this a very satisfying example of a formal, geometrical patio pond. It is the sense of balance and proportion that makes an immediate appeal.*

Glazed tiles and to a lesser extent smooth-faced bricks will tend to give your patio garden an atmosphere of coolness. In warm climates this may be exactly what you want. In more temperate zones, the same tiles may create a sense of coldness rather than coolness. And glazed tiles, while attractive in themselves, give the impression of being slippery, which indeed they may be, especially when wet. Remember too that tiles have to be laid on a very smooth and firm foundation; any bumps or aberrations are very obvious in a tiled patio. Embossed tiles or bricks which have been given a slightly roughened appearance in production — often called rustic bricks — help create a warmer and I think more welcoming environment. Bricks are adaptable and look well in any size of garden, although there is a great deal of work involved in laying them.

Concrete slabs are available in all sorts of shapes and sizes, and square, rectangular, octagonal and hexagonal slabs are all popular.

28

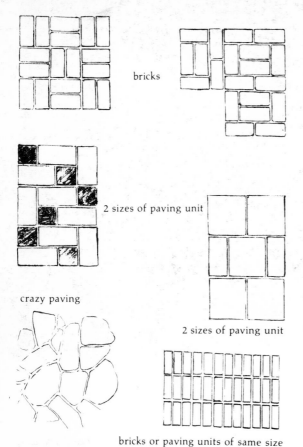

bricks

2 sizes of paving unit

crazy paving

2 sizes of paving unit

bricks or paving units of same size

A variety of paving patterns

And they can be laid quickly and easily. Their bold and individual outlines may, however, come across as too strong and marked in a small garden. Match the size of your paving elements to the size of your garden: the larger your patio, the larger can be the elements.

If you find the patio a little on the stark side, the effect can easily be softened, not only by growing shrubs in large pots or tubs, but by planting directly in the patio. Just lift out a whole slab if you are using large paving elements, and plant the shrub in good quality soil. If your patio consists of small pavers laid on sand, then the pavers making up the perimeter of the planting square will have to be set in mortar on top of a concrete footing

about 10 cm. thick. Box and Sweet Bay make fine evergreen shrubs for a patio and can be clipped to whatever size or shape you want. For a more formal effect you could choose those marvellously thin, slender and compact *scopulorum* Junipers, one planted at each corner of the pond. They would provide a great depth to the garden by their reflection in the water. But remember not to make conditions cramped on the patio by injudicious planting.

Raised beds offer another, and greatly underrated, possibility. The walls of the beds could be made from a contrasting material; the patio might be made of concrete and the beds of brick, or one might use two different tones of concrete. A different tile, brick or whatever, might be used as a surround to the pond to highlight it as the central feature. Contrasting colours can, of course, be used as 'veins' in the pattern of the patio, but without an experienced eye such attempts may turn out woefully fussy and over done. Simplicity is no sin.

Informal ponds

And simplicity is certainly no sin in the design of a formal pond. For it is precisely by its broad sweeps and well defined lines that a formal water scheme makes its appeal. And the same applies to informal ponds. Here one is not aiming at geometric clarity; but a natural water scheme is quite different from a chaotic one, and it is achieved by simple, well-laid out plantings and groupings of plants. The question is when to opt for a formal pond and when an informal one. Personal taste is likely to be the first consideration, but the layout of your garden as it already exists needs to be taken into consideration. By and large, a highly formalized garden with trees, shrubs and hedges and particularly paths laid out with geometric precision, demands a pond of equal precision. As a general rule the lines of the pond should conform with the lines of

A beautifully secluded woodland pool.

the adjacent hedges or walls. The overall geometric layout must be one of harmony. Strong lines that do not run parallel or are not laid out at very definite angles will look awful.

That said, geometric and formal lines are more easily destroyed than created. Should you inherit a formal garden and wish to alter it, nothing could be easier. The severity of a hedge can be softened by the planting of shrubs at various places along its length. A geometric border can be made into an informal one, simply by cutting out curved sections along its edge. An informal pond, if combined with a rockery, is not so likely to clash with an otherwise formal garden. If you create a rockery, make sure the rocks or boulders you use are buried in the soil to at least half their height, preferably more. You might think it a waste of rock and effort to conceal it. But a rock simply stuck on top of the soil looks very unnatural.

Waterfalls

A rockery opens up the possibility of including a waterfall and stream into your scheme. If the rockery is made from newly dug ground make sure you compact the course of the stream, particularly where you intend having the waterfall, otherwise subsidence may result. Large-scale water courses (that is to say streams and waterfalls composed of rocks or boulders larger than you can move by hand) need to have a foundation of hard core, as large boulders will inevitably sink if laid on soft earth.

Instant waterfalls and small streams are to be had by buying glass fibre 'dishes' and 'stream sections'. There is no doubt that some manufacturers of glass fibre rocks and boulders produce very realistic results, although the majority of miniature streams made for the domestic market are less satisfactory, and some glass fibre watercourses sold in garden centres would not deceive the eye for a minute. Still, a brisk trade appears to be done in such things.

If you want to make your own watercourse with real rocks and gravel, bed down the rock elements on a bed or mortar under which has been laid a flexible membrane. For a stream, cut out the meandering shape you want, lay down a bed of sand, then the liner and finally the rocks. The procedure is really the same as for building a pond. Remember to allow for the width of the rocks along either side of the stream. For example, if the rocks are roughly 25 cm. wide and you want the water in the stream to be 60 cm. wide, then your excavation must be 1.10 metres wide, which will look enormous until you complete the stream, when it may appear quite small by comparison. Add a few rocks along the centre of the watercourse, or off centre, for added realism; at any rate try to avoid two stiff lines for the banks. Mix the sizes of rock you use and vary their position. Rocks in a well-designed stream or waterfall should look as if 'they had always been there.'

When it comes to making a waterfall you will, of course, need height and a rock which has a suitable 'lip' or sill over which the water will pour. A good waterfall designer can 'read' a rock and will know what kind of effect any given rock will provide. Generally speaking, the sharper the edge of the stone the 'cleaner' will be the fall of water. A piece of slate, for example (though not necessarily the most natural of stones for a waterfall), will provide a sheet of falling water, whereas a stone with rough edges will provide a broken effect. If the stone or rock has a rounded sill the water will tend to follow the curve, and in the absence of sufficient velocity may do no more than dribble. If you want the water to shoot off the sill, find a means of suddenly increasing the velocity of the water, which is simple enough to do: narrow the space behind the

waterfall sill. The water then has to pick up speed as it goes through the smaller space.

It is not easy to judge suitable waterfall stones without experience, but remember two things: choose a stone with a flat surface and make sure that it is *perfectly level crosswise*. If it is not, if it tips only slightly to one side the water will not spread evenly over the sill. What if your rock does not have a perfectly level and smooth surface? Then you must try to take an average reading and balance out the bumps and hollows. Remember, too, to incline the waterfall rock slightly forward if your want to get a clean pour. If you want turbulence and the effect that is sometimes described as 'white water', then place some obstructions behind the waterfall. Obstructions and hollows will create turbulence during which air is drawn into the water. The effect is white water. Refraction in falling water has a similar effect, so that rough or 'toothed' sills are sometimes used (made by chipping out nicks with a cold chisel) for this purpose.

Waterfalls and streams are nearly always powered by submersible pumps. All you need in addition to the pump is a non-return valve (sometimes called a check valve) to prevent water from the stream returning to the pond

A waterfall can be powered as illustrated, with a submersible pump placed in the pond close to the waterfall. Keep the pump clear of the mud by supporting on bricks.

when your pump is turned off, and a length of flexible hose going from the pump to the top of the stream or waterfall (see drawing). A qualified electrician should make the electrical connection, preferably using a ground fault interrupter or leak switch for safety (in fact such may be a legal requirement under certain circumstances). Land pumps are generally used now only for water displays of really massive size. Although the pump itself might cost less than a submersible of the same power, the additional plumbing is costly and time consuming (see drawing), and if the pump is higher than the pond there can be a problem in keeping it primed. A footvalve is required, and can leak if it becomes clogged.

In order to keep the disturbance of water lilies to a minimum, it is usual to site the submersible pump right under the waterfall. It is not usual to place the pump at the far end of the pool, but I have found that by doing this the flow of water through the underwater plants can be an excellent way of clearing the water of suspended mud and detritus. Such an arrangement is not ideal for permanently running water, but can work well if you use your waterfall only occasionally. The cost of running a submersible pump has to be borne in mind.

What should be the flow rate of the submersible pump you choose? As a rule of thumb 1200 US gallons (1000 Imp. gallons) or 4500 litres per hour will provide a tinkling waterfall, if the sill is about 12 inches or 30 cm. across. Double that flow rate and you will get something more turbulent. Another way of approaching the question is to consider the head of water a given flow rate will provide above a given sill length. Here are some calculations:

Head	25cm. sill	50 cm. sill	75 cm. sill
1 cm	1800 litres	3240 litres	5040 l. per hour
1.5	2880	6120	9000
2.00	4680	9360	14000

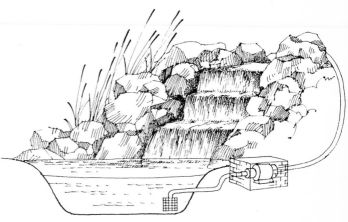

A land pump must be set in a weatherproof structure with ventilation, or the motor may overheat. A foot-valve must be attached to the inlet pipe, or water will flow back from the waterfall when the pump is turned off.

These figures are intended to be no more than a guideline, as the nature of the rockface and other factors will influence the result.

The higher the waterfall is above the surface of the pond (which is known as the head of water), the more work your pump will have to do and the smaller will be its output. For example, a pump might be capable of delivering 3000 litres per hour at a 1 metre head, but only 1800 litres at 2 metres. Refer to the performance graph of pumps in order to

Graph showing comparative performance, in metres/feet and US gallons/litres, of a waterfall and a fountain pump. The output of the waterfall pump is much greater, but declines relatively quickly in relation to head of water. The fountain pump has a lower output but is less affected by the head.

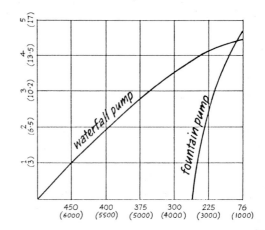

get what you want. A waterfall pump is usually designed to deliver large volumes at comparatively low heads of water, whereas a fountain pump, which must operate under the constraint of a narrow nozzle, is usually designed to provide a comparatively low volume of water under high pressure. Using the right pump for the job is more economical where running costs are concerned.

In addition to the head of water, you should bear in mind that there will be a certain amount of friction loss depending upon the length of the pipe you are using, its bore and its bends. Large-scale water works have these friction losses worked out mathematically.

There is a water feature to suit every situation. The dramatic waterfall was designed for an hotel. BELOW LEFT *A bubbling stream makes a child-safe feature.* BELOW *A pond and fountain will make an elegant centrepiece in any garden.*

Wrought ironwork and the fountain combine to make a fine image. Where enclosed and patio ponds are concerned, wrought iron can be used to great effect.

For a garden pond you should perhaps allow a friction loss of about 15 per cent. That, of course, is only the roughest guide, and if at all possible use an outlet pipe that is larger than the outlet of the pump. In other words, if the pump outlet thread is 2.0 cm. then use a 2.5 or 3 cm. outlet pipe. That will make a significant difference to the flow rate.

Choosing a pump for a fountain is an easier business, as fountain jets usually come with a recommendation as to the power required to operate them. If in doubt use the advice of a water specialist who will be familiar with the intricacies of pump design and performance. Fountain nozzles are produced in a vast range of styles and sizes. The nozzle is generally attached to a rigid length of pipe which can be cut so that the jet stands just proud of the water surface, while the submersible pump is stood on blocks directly beneath. Always keep submersible pumps clear of the floor of the pond to prevent mulm entering the inlet chamber.

Water in motion raises the oxygen level in a pond, so fish will appreciate a fountain or waterfall. Unfortunately water lilies will not. They like neither being continually dowsed in water, which will make them close up and sink, nor perpetual currents. So far as a fountain is concerned, unless your pond is large enough to accommodate one in one area and the water lilies in another, they make poor companions. And a common mistake is to have the jet of water too high for the size of pond in which it is installed. The slightest breeze carries the jet over the bank and in no time the water level sinks. As a rule of thumb the jet should reach no higher than half the width of the pond, in other words a jet 2 metres high would need a pond at least 4

BELOW *A fountain pump with synthetic foam fitted over the inlet. The effect of foam (or synthetic sponge, as it is also called) of this size would be primarily mechanical rather than biological in its filtration performance.*

metres wide. A wind responder can be installed in line with the electric lead, which will automatically reduce the height of the fountain according to the wind level.

For rocks to look natural they must be partially buried in the soil.

Rockeries

A useful way of dealing with the spoil that comes from excavating a site for a pond is to make a rockery with it. Thought should be given to how the rockery stones are placed. A common mistake is to leave the stones or boulders on top of the rockery, but nothing looks less natural. Nature buries rocks, sometimes a third is below ground level, often half and maybe more. It may seem an awful waste of effort hauling a huge boulder half-way round a garden and half-way up a rockery, only to bury the greater part of it, but if you are after a natural result, if you want the boulder to look as if 'it had always been there', then that is the way to deal with it.

Secondly, think of rock groups. There is no question that odd numbers make for better rock groupings than even numbers. Occasionally, if you have a very special stone, it may look best on its own, but generally you should think in terms of groups of three or five, not of two or four. The experienced handler of rock will immediately have a sense of the grain and rhythm of the stones. There is such a thing as placing a rock upside down — again the experienced eye will detect it; and once you have become accustomed to looking at rocks, one laid upside down just looks wrong and that's the end of the matter. Similarly, the elements in a rock grouping will have a much greater chance of appearing in harmony if

their shapes relate to one another. If this seems mystifying at first it becomes less so with practice. Take the following three examples. In the first a large stone is clearly a vertical. It can be complemented by a lower stone, and the obvious place in which to fit it is in the side which appears slightly concave. As the vertical also has a 'toe', try to line up a stone with the rhythm that this feature portrays. Always try to combine stones by fitting them together; a rounded stone may fit a smooth concave area of another but would look quite wrong if placed against a jagged edged rock. On the other hand you may be able to combine two rocks with sharp edges. The stones do not have to interlock like dovetail joints, they only have to complement each other. Nearly every rock has several faces, usually one which is bad and can be put on the blind side, and the other faces will vary in size and shape, so you are offered choices. Another point worth remembering is that a rock often combines best with one that is unlike it in regard to size and shape, so a 'vertical' might combine best with a 'flat'. If you have a mind to it, rockery building can be planned in miniature with nothing more than a sand tray and pieces of random aggregate.

The current fashion is for informal, natural water schemes rather than formal ones. But to make an artificial watercourse look natural and give the impression 'that it was always there' is by no means as easy as it might seem. The rocks and stones must be carefully selected and placed. This picture shows what can be achieved by a master of his craft.

Bridges

A bridge can add as much to a garden pond as a waterfall. The pond needs to be designed so that it narrows at some point, preferably somewhere near the middle, and there the bridge can be spanned. If the pond is of much the same width throughout, a bridge may look out of place. Probably the easiest kind of bridge to make is a wooden one. Two strong beams are placed side by side to span the channel. They can be secured by burying in concrete. Planks are then cut and screwed into the beams at right angles. The width of a bridge should be at least 60 cm. for convenience. A concrete bridge is almost as simple. Make a wooden 'trough' — which can be easily dismantled — and lay it across the channel. Fill with concrete and reinforcement. The sides and top surface can easily be faced with stones or paving slabs. The thickness of the bridge will depend upon its length and the weight it must carry.

For foot traffic over curved or flat concrete bridges these figures represent the minimum reinforcement and thickness of concrete required.

It is important, to avoid cracking, that the bars are embedded in the lower third of the concrete and this must be well compacted. At the same time ensure that there is 25 mm. or more of concrete below each bar.

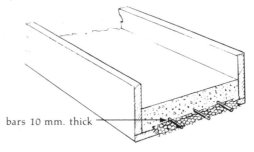

bars 10 mm. thick

Dressed stone in an arched bridge adds a formal touch in an informal setting.

An arched bridge requires a great deal more effort and skill. For this, one has to build an arched frame made of wood. Plywood bent over a series of formers is probably the simplest method of making such a frame. This must span the channel precisely and just come in contact with two concrete foundations set in the soil on either side. The foundations should be slightly lower than the soil so that they are not visible. The concrete for the arch will need to be made fairly firm, otherwise when you lay it on the wooden frame it will part in the middle and slump down on either side. The value of the foundations is that they will act as a buffer to the

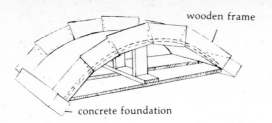

wooden frame

concrete foundation

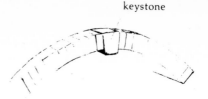

keystone

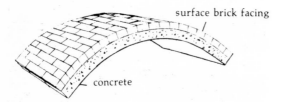

surface brick facing

concrete

gap cut in frame for keystone

frame pulled out to support facing bricks

Method of constructing an arched bridge comprising of concrete and bricks. Considerable skill is needed to produce a workmanlike result.

bridge as it sets. It would not be impossible, however, to construct the bridge without them. Simply dig out the soil on either side of the pond to receive the bridge and do the concreting in one job. Work is made much easier if the curve of the arch is not too great. It also means the bridge will be easier to walk over. A concrete arched bridge can be very effectively faced with bricks. One course of bricks is laid cross-wise over the top of the concrete form. Two further courses are arranged in 'fan shape' on either face of the bridge. (The inclusion of a larger key-stone adds a tremendous amount to the appearance of a bridge, if you can get one made.) Once the concrete part of the bridge is quite hard, you can face its top surface and then carry out the fan work as follows. Take off the side of the frame which was used to hold in the wet concrete. Move out the wooden frame on one side of the bridge to the width of one brick. The bricks can then be supported by the frame until the whole arch is completed, when it becomes self supporting. If a large keystone is being used, you may have to cut out a space in the wooden frame to accommodate its

greater length. Having done one side, the frame can then be pushed through the bridge to appear on the other side, and the second set of bricks is cemented in place. To start this 'fan work' it is important to have two concrete foundations finished *at such an angle* that the fan of bricks can be started directly against them. A bridge of this kind does need a certain standard of craftsmanship. Any part of it which is not quite right will show up badly. But such a bridge offers great opportunities for individual touches of design and the results can be very satisfying.

Cost

How much might a pond cost? Like almost any building project, there is no ceiling to what one can pay. But water gardening can certainly be regarded as an inexpensive pastime. An attractive, moderate-sized pond is within the reach of anyone. I would suggest, however, that you avoid the cheaper types of liner. Using polythene is false economy. If you do decide on a liner pond, it is only wise to buy the best, that is the heavier grade of Butyl rubber or PVC with nylon laminate. All these liners cost much the same and their cost is similar to that of concrete (excluding the additional labour involved.) Fibreglass or plastic ponds run at about three times the price of concrete and liner ponds. Taken as an example, a modest sized pond, say 1.8 x 1.2 x 0.75 metres deep, would require a stretchable liner 3.3 x 2.7 metres or 0.76 cubic metres of concrete. There is no point in giving the actual monetary cost of such a pond, since inflation is likely to make nonsense of the figure within a short time. But one can give a comparative value. Such a medium-priced pond would cost roughly the same as a man's sports jacket. Adding a submersible pump would more or less double the price. The cost of liners rises in proportion to their increase in size. The price of pumps increases by between 50 and 75 per cent as their output doubles.

The addition of a patio would be your largest single cost. For the pond in question, one would need a patio at least 5.4 x 3.6 metres: 19.44 sq. metres. Pre-cast concrete slabs are

Stepping stones make a very attractive feature in a water scheme, and of course children love to use them.

A devilish fountain mask gushing forth water in three jets. Wall fountains of this kind with a tiny pond beneath are a clever way of decorating a small area.

among the cheapest kinds of paving units. Using 60 cm. square slabs, one would need a total of 48 slabs, i.e. (19.44 - 2.16) ÷ 0.36. Roughly speaking, 50 concrete slabs would cost about the same as the liner and pump combined. So as a guide to the cost of a small patio pond, one could say it would be the equivalent of two sports jackets and one medium-priced suit. Clothes vary in price of course. But this comparision indicates the sort of money one is talking about.

Your new pond, freshly filled with water, will have a crystal clarity. But as you will discover, that state will not last. Quickly or slowly, the water will discolour until it becomes a murky green. The process is inevitable. But no less inevitable is the process by which this state is reversed. Without changing the water, the original clarity can be regained permanently. Having built your pond, the next step is the judicious planting of underwater plants.

41

3   THE SECRET OF CLEAR WATER

A beautifully planted, small tropical pond.

Water turns green because the mineral salts it contains, the sunlight it absorbs and the carbon dioxide given off by fish and pond animals, are just what the minute spores of green algae need to exist and multiply. When present in their millions, these tiny organisms clutter the water to such an extent that everything else in the pool is invisible. Changing the water is no more than a temporary solution because the process will immediately begin all over again, and in any case water lilies require undisturbed water. The pond looks hopelessly polluted when vast amounts of algae are present, although, in fact, they are not harmful to fish who will happily feed off these organisms. Algae are simply unsightly.

The answer to clearing a pond of algae, or at least to radically reducing their number, is to starve them of their needs. Underwater plants (or oxygenating plants, as aquarists call them) will fulfil this function. Actually to describe underwater plants as oxygenators is really only to describe half their function, and not the most important one. Oxygen is absorbed by water through surface contact with the surrounding air, underwater plants merely add to that process. But they also absorb the carbon dioxide and mineral salts essential to algae. And once the underwater plants have appropriated all the available food, the algae, in the unequal struggle for survival, simply die, and the pond becomes crystal clear. Do bear in mind, however, that between filling the pond with water and the establishment of oxygenating plants, algae will thrive. A 'pea soup' period has to be endured in the confidence that if you have a sufficient number of underwater plants they will win in the end, and the algae will be reduced, as one writer so brightly put it: 'to a fine shower of corpses'.

With only temporary lapses, the water should remain permanently clear. The lapses are most likely to occur in spring after a sudden spell of warm, sunny weather. The algae will immediately start into growth and conditions will be favourable to them. During the dormant winter period there will have been a build up of waste animal matter. The pond will be in a eutrophic or nutrient-rich condition and this state will remain until the oxygenating plants are again growing actively. Then the pond will return to a comparatively oligotrophic or mineral-deficient condition and the water will clear. It is surprising how quickly the change occurs. One day you may be glumly looking at the 'soup' and the next into water almost as transparent as a mountain stream. (It should be noted however that while underwater plants can reduce the growth of most algae, what is known as filamentous algae or blanket weed — which looks and feels a bit like green cotton-wool — can thrive even in oligotrophic conditions, and when it appears it really needs to be removed by hand, or by being twirled round the end of a stick.)

The small, three-petalled white flower of Elodea densa is the surest way of identifying it.

The secret of clear water

It is impossible to say what amount of underwater plants any particular pond needs. The factors are far too complex and variable. They would include the amount of sunlight the pool receives, the depth and temperature of the water, its mineral and animal content and much more. But it can be said that all underwater plants will carry out the dual function of removing carbon dioxide and adding oxygen to the water. Their presence is absolutely essential to clear water unless you install a filtration system (dealt with in Chapter 8). As a rule of thumb — and it is no more than that — if a third of the total volume of the pool appears to contain oxygenators, then that should be sufficient. From the point of view of maintaining clear water, your pond cannot have too many underwater plants. However, there is one respect in which underwater plants can prove a hazard, and that is to fish. While these plants absorb carbon dioxide and give off oxygen during the day, at night, in the absence of sunlight, the same plants give off carbon dioxide. Under very still, humid conditions, the surface of the pond may not be able to take in sufficient oxygen for the needs of the fish, which could then suffocate. The warning signs to be seen at night or early morning are the fish coming up to the surface and gasping, mouth and gills working in a slow rhythm, a rhythm that is more emphatic than when the fish come to the surface simply to feed. There is a simple answer to this hazard. Water in motion readily collects oxygen, and even a small rippling effect on a limited area of the surface of your pond will enable the water to absorb oxygen in humid, thundery weather when 'there isn't a breath about.' A waterfall or fountain will do this very well.

Propagation of oxygenators is simple. All that is required is to snip off the top few centimetres of a stem. Stick this in the soil and it will develop quite happily. Alternatively, a whole plant with its roots can be weighted

Elodea canadensis – Canadian Pondweed or Ditch Moss

down with a piece of lead and simply dropped into the pond to root naturally on the bottom. Strips cut from an empty tooth-paste tube make good weights. All underwater plants reproduce vegetatively and they can often be divided up after only a couple of months. Instead of laying down a layer of soil over the whole base of the pond, it is now common practice to grow plants in shallow containers. When the pond is made of concrete either way is possible. Liner pools require the use of containers because stones contained in a layer of soil might puncture the liner, should the stones get scattered on the base of the pond and then get trodden on. In fact gravel (pea gravel is safest, having round and smooth surfaces) is often used instead of soil, as your underwater plants will take their nutrition from the surrounding water primarily through their leaves. Oxygenators grown in containers will very soon creep over the sides and root themselves in any debris on the bottom. So when you want to reduce their number, all you have to do is remove the baskets, take out all the surplus weed in the bottom of the pond and then return the containers. Most oxygenators will quickly take over the pond, so containers are a useful way of keeping them in check.

Many ponds are oxygenated and purified by one or more of the Elodeas. The North American Water Thyme or Ditch Moss, *Elodea canadensis (Anacharis)* is an excellent purifier but also a most vigorous one especially outside its native habitat. It may have been recorded in Ireland in the 1830's and reached England in the early 1840's. But the most celebrated transference of the plant occurred in 1847-8, when the Curator of the Botanic Gardens at Cambridge, England, received specimens of the plant from a Professor Babington and placed them in a tributary of the River Cam. Within a few years the plant had monopolized huge stretches of the Cam, making swimming and boating all but impossible, and actually raising the level of the river. The weed became known as 'Babington's Curse'. Its prodigious ability to spread was carried out purely vegetatively, as only female strands of the plant had been imported. *E. canadensis* caused the same problem in other places where it was planted or transferred. Then after some years its vigour, for some reason, declined and the plant became a civil enough member of the plant community. When introduced to 'new' water it does seem to regain some of its lost vigour and may not settle down for some years, though this is not invariably the case. When I first used the plant I found my pond was very quickly taken over. Then after about five years its rate of reproduction seemed to slow down. In other instances this species grows quite modestly. You are very likely to find that if you introduce, say, three different underwater species into your pond, one may take off while the growth of the other two remains fairly modest; then, after a few seasons, the prolific one may become less vigorous and instead one of the other two becomes dominant. Change of this kind is common: A pond is not the static, unchanging environment you might expect it to be. If your pond is small and it can be readily swept by hand, *E. canadensis* will be manageable no matter how vigorous. What you take out makes a fine fertiliser, and if you keep a compost heap (as every gardener should to re-cycle kitchen waste and other biodegradable material), you can add *Anacharis* or any other aquatic vegetation to the compost heap. It is when one has a large watercourse that one has to be careful about what plants are introduced, as maintenance can then become a serious problem.

For large ponds, you could use *Elodea densa (Egeria densa)* which is also an excellent oxygenator while being less prolific. The two plants are very similar in appearance and they are not easy to distinguish. The easiest way of identifying them is through their flowers. *Densa* throws up conspicuous three-petalled white flowers above the surface, whereas if *canadensis* flowers at all, it will have tiny pink or white flowers, floating on the surface on the ends of long strands. The leaves of *canadensis* are produced in whorls of three or four and each leaf is usually minutely toothed. (You may need a magnifying lens to make out the teeth.) Leaves of *densa* are tooth-

Callitriche stagnalis – Water Starwort

less or nearly so and produced in crowded whorls. And there are usually four leaves to each whorl. In a mature plant the leaves will be 2.5 cm. long at least, whereas the leaves of *canadensis* should be a great deal less than that. *Elodea callitrichoides* is larger than the other two, having leaves over 3 cm. long in whorls of three or occasionally two. *Elodea crispa (Lagarosiphon major)*, which has alternate leaves about 3 cm. long, is more suited to the aquarium than the outdoor pond as it is not fully hardy. Incidentally, when identifying these plants, bear in mind that considerable variation occurs from locality to locality. The length of leaves, for example, can vary greatly.

Although there may be an abundance of water weeds growing wild in rivers, lakes or streams near where you live, it is not advisable to take your stock from such sources, especially if you are not absolutely certain of the identity of the plants in question. You could be taking — and depleting — rare plants protected by law; and in fact in some countries it is against the law to take any plants from the wild, rare or otherwise. (What is common today may be rare in ten years time.) Secondly, you could be introducing unwanted parasites into your pond from the wild, parasites or their eggs which remain hidden among the leaves. Aquatic nurseries and garden centres can supply you with all the water plants you need. Moreover many underwater plants are notoriously difficult to identify (and let it be said that classification of underwater plants is neither exhaustive nor always clear); but all plants that produce underwater leaves (as opposed to those whose leaves begin underwater only to rise above it later on), will function as water purifiers. Some oxygenators can adapt themselves to both running and still water, while others are capable of surviving in one situation only. Obviously you should concentrate on those species that favour still water conditions.

The Callitriches comprise a large genus that one is certain to find in the wild. The Common Water-Starwort, *Callitriche stagnalis,* is to be found throughout much of Europe. It is well suited to cold water but not to warm, hence its absence from Mediterranean areas and from indoor aquariums. It has a preference for shallow water and will continue to grow during the winter — a useful feature. So too will the Autumnal Starwort, *C. autumnalis,* which, however, is not fussy about temperatures. It also has the advantage of not breaking the surface, a feature shared by the Hornworts, *Ceratophyllum demersum* and *submersum.* If you have a deep pool, *demersum* is a particularly good choice as it will fill whatever depth is provided for it. The Willow Moss, *Fontinalis antipyretica*, is another excellent oxygenator and a beautiful one into the bargain. It has long foliage, not unlike seaweed, but of a rich, vivid green. Obtain a whole plant with the roots intact if you can. It is more likely to be found in running water, attached to a rock or stone, than in still water. As the name *anti-*

One of the sub-species of Ranunculus aquatilis, the Water Crowfoot. It produces a mass of small but showy white flowers during the summer.

Ceratophyllum demersum — Hornwort

pyretica might imply, it is non-combustible and was once used as a form of fire insulation between chimneys and walls.

If you like the idea of including an oxygenator with attractive flowers held well above the surface, then one can hardly do better than to obtain the Water Violet, *Hottonia palustris*, which produces whorls of light purple or sometimes white flowers. In the American form, *Hottonia inflata*, the flowers are always white. The Water Violet is not always an easy plant to get established. Featherfoil is another name for the plant, not to be confused with Parrot's Feather, which is the common name of *Myriophyllum prosperpinacoides*. One can hardly regard this lovely plant as an ideal underwater plant since it likes nothing better than to rise out of the water and, given the opportunity, hang gracefully over the edge of a bank or side of an aquarium. It has been used on occasions in hanging baskets filled with water, so that the finely cut leaves and the gorgeous light green colour of the plant appears right before one's eyes. The lovely feathery foliage, as well as the colour,

certainly justifies such treatment, and Parrot's Feather is well worth including in the pond if only for its ornamental value. It does need to be wintered indoors as it is not fully hardy. Spiked Water Milfoil, *Myriophyllum spicatum*, has feathery foliage too, and is one of the most beautiful of underwater plants. It is quite hardy and common in many waterways in Europe. *Myriophyllum* is dark green, as is *Ceratophyllum* (Hornwort) and at a distance they look rather similar. But Hornwort is bristly to the touch, the leaves remaining stiff when you take the plant out of the water, whereas Milfoil is soft to the touch and goes limp out of water. Hornwort, incidentally, has no roots and bits simply dropped into the pond will grow where they lie. In summer it sends up very small but nonetheless conspicuous red and yellow flowers, which is an added bonus in a plant which is an excellent purifier. *Myriophyllum verticillatum* is found in North America and Australia as well as Europe, favouring warmer water than *M. spicatum*. Its flowers are insignificant.

Myriophyllum prosperpinacoides — Parrot's Feather

BELOW *The Water Violet, Hottonia palustris. The plant is not, in fact, related to the Violet but to the Primrose family. The name 'violet' comes from the colour of the flowers.*

For a mass of white buttercup-shaped flowers floating or just raised above the surface, grow the Water Crowfoot or *Ranunculus aquatilis*. It is a good example of how adaptable nature can be. The plant has two distinct kinds of leaves. Those under water are finely divided, which enables the functions of collecting carbon dioxide and giving off oxygen to be carried out efficiently. The leaves on the surface are not more than deeply lobed and are, of course, quite flat so that the leaves can float and maintain their equilibrium. A carpet of Water Crowfoot running the length of the bank is an attractive feature in spring when the flowers appear. If

you want to use it as an oxygenator, plant it in reasonably deep water otherwise the underwater leaves may not develop. Another conspicuous hardy underwater plant is *Potamogeton crispus*, or Curled Pondweed, which is easily recognised by its broad, buckled and crimped leaves of bronze hue, or dark green if grown in shade. It can be a vigorous species, and like Hornwort is much favoured by goldfish for the deposition of their eggs.

In the United States *Cambomba caroliniana* is a particularly popular pond and aquarium plant. It has narrow floating leaves and fan shaped, narrow underwater leaves. It is sometimes called Fanwort or Washington Grass. A bonus in growing this plant is to be had in the attractive white flowers, each sepal of which has a conspicuous yellow spot. *C. aquatica* has similar foliage, somewhat denser, and yellow flowers. It favours warmer water and is rather more tender than *C. caroliniana*, but neither species can be regarded as hardy. Nor is *Lasarosiphon major* (*Elodea crispa*), which looks a bit like a big version of *Elodea canadensis* except that the leaves have a rather curly appearance. It is a strong growing plant, and will often survive outdoors in the UK in winter, but if you want to be certain of having some in the spring, then winter it indoors in an aquarium. And talking of aquarium plants, probably no species has been grown more widely than *Vallisneria spiralis*, or Ribbon Grass, with its long, strap-like leaves and light green foliage. *V. americana* is also pale green, but may be identified by having spots of a purplish hue and sometimes, in the case of older foliage, yellow markings running along the leaf. *Vallisneria* is easily propagated by means of runners which will proliferate once the plant is established in your pond or aquarium. *V. americana* is a tropical plant and *V. spiralis*, though it may live in a cold water pond in mild areas, is not fully hardy. Occasionally in the UK you may come across the astonishing sight of *Vallisneria* thriving in open water —

where it has found an industry discharging warm water. Such stands are the result of a 'garden or aquarium escape', someone having simply thrown out plants surplus to their needs. In tropical areas, there is a higher level of concern about such practice, as a so-called garden escape can dramatically change the ecology of an area in a short time. In the United States it is forbidden to bring certain plants across state borders. In temperate zones the effects are less obvious, if only because the speed of change is less rapid and the clogging of waterways less of a problem. Nevertheless, throwing out plants or introducing new plants to established waterways is to be avoided.

The question of the pH of pond water, its 'hardness' or 'softness', how acid or alkaline it should be, is sometimes raised; and underwater plants are affected by, and in their turn, affect pH values. The pH scale, used internationally, is a means of measuring the degree to which water (or soil) is acid or alkaline. A value of 7 is regarded as neutral; if your pond water has a value below 7 then it is acidic, whereas if it has a reading above 7 it is alkaline. If the pH of your pool lies somewhere between roughly 6.2 and 7.4, then you should encounter no problems in growing most pond plants. Unless you have reason to believe that the water you will be using to fill and maintain the water in your pond is extremely acidic, or very alkaline, there is no need to take any action. If in doubt you can test the water with a simple pH kit. This consists of comparing a sample of water mixed with an indicator liquid, or pH paper (wetted in the pond water), against a colour chart. If the test paper or liquid turns red, then the pH reading will be around 4.5 and means the water is very acid indeed. At the other end of the scale, dark blue indicates alkalinity; and green shows the neutral range of 6.4 to 7. What to do if your pond water is at one of the extremes? Underwater plants will tend to 'pull' the water

towards the mean, provided, of course, that they can establish themselves. This assumes that your pond is a still-water one, a closed-system, in which 'new' water is introduced only to top it up. If you have water flowing through your pond, as from a stream for example, then the pH is likely to remain much the same in the pond as the stream. Most plants grow in conditions which are on the alkaline side. *Elodea canadensis* (*Anacharis*) and *Egeria densa* will do in water which has a pH even as high as 10; and Hornwort (*Ceratophyllum*) and Milfoil (*Myriophyllum*) like a fairly high pH value, being most vigorous when the water has a high calcium content. *Potamogeton crispus* prefers a more neutral pH, while *Vallisneria spiralis* and *V. americana* like water which is mildly acidic, as does *Cambomba aquatica*. It is where the only source of water for your pond is very acid — has a very low pH value — that you might have trouble getting pond plants established. If you could tap a rain water tank, that would be one way of resolving your problem; or you could try a very dense planting of underwater plants in

Lemna minor – Lesser Duckweed

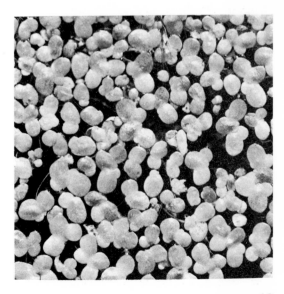

the hope that sheer numbers will raise the pH quickly. Failing that, it is possible to alter the pH of water by means of chemicals, such are available under brand names like Alkaplus and Alkaminus, the first to raise the pH in your pond, the second to lower it.

So-called floating plants, those which for at least part of the year live on the surface of the pond, are not effective as oxygenators. But they do play a part in keeping the water clear in so far as they cut down the amount of sunlight the algae receive and by using some of the nutrients in the pond. They are primarily grown for their ornamental value. The Common Duckweed, *Lemna minor*, is a very familiar sight: those little bright green discs which cover many a wild pond and ditch. Fish may enjoy it, but it is rather prolific and if you introduce it into your pond, you may involve yourself in tiresome thinning-out op-

Azolla — Water Fern

BELOW *Trapa natans*

A striking display of the Water Soldier, Stratiotes aloides.

wide area. It has long been popular as an aquarium plant and seems to be increasingly popular for the outdoor pond. *S. auriculata* is similar, although the leaves are flatter. *Salvinia* probably does best in dappled shade, as does the water fern or water sprite, *Ceratopteris thalictroides*, which is found in several forms. Grown on the base of the pond it will produce fronds that are divided and rather fern-like (especially *forma Cornuta*), and on the surface it will grow in rosette form. It favours warm, acid water, and is often grown as an annual.

Rather like a miniature water lily is Frogbit, *Hydrocharis morsus-ranae*, which has light green, round to kidney-shaped leaves not much larger than a thumb nail, and little white flowers. In winter the plant dies off but not before producing terminal buds which become separated from the parent plant to lie on the bottom of the pool until the following spring. Of similar habit is the Water Soldier, *Stratiotes aloides*, which only makes a brief appearance on the

erations. The same is true for all the Lemnas with one notable exception. That is *Lemna trisulca*, the Ivy-Leaved Duckweed. It consists of oval or elliptical fronds of a greeny transparency, and the fronds are linked together by thin strands. If you have experienced trouble in keeping your pond clear, get hold of this duckweed, it is excellent for purifying water. If you have seen the Fairy Moss, *Azolla caroliniana,* you are bound to have been struck by its delicate tones of green in summer and vivid red in autumn. It is, without doubt, a beautiful plant; but be warned, it is not simply prolific but can take over a pond in the manner of a wall-to-wall carpet. So thorough is the Fairy Moss in covering the surface of a pool that it has been used in Panama and elsewhere to prevent mosquitoes laying their eggs in the water. *Salvinia braziliensis* is another tiny floating plant from tropical America, each plant being smaller than a finger-nail, though it can be prolific and spread over a

RIGHT *Eichhornia crassipes*

Hydrocharis morsus-ranae – Frogbit

surface and looks like the top of a large pine-apple. For most of the time the Water Soldier is submerged. Like the Frogbit, it produces side shoots or bulblets which lie dormant until the spring and the mature plants only appear to produce their white flowers. The plants then sink back again. *Stratiotes aloides* is calcareous, that is to say it prefers limestone waters. And this may explain why it does not always transfer readily. On the other hand, it can be prolific; but the plants are so large (30 cm.

A mature specimen of the Water Lettuce, Pistia stratiotes with two or three young plants appearing as side shoots.

across) that they can easily be removed by hand as necessary.

Many water gardeners, living outside the tropics or sub-tropical zones, treat tender aquatics as annuals, buying in new stock each year. But if you have a glass house or conservatory, or an aquarium, it is fun to try to overwinter plants. You could try with the most beautiful of all floating plants, the Water Hyacinth, *Eichhornia crassipes* (*speciosa*) — see p. 51. I say try because it really needs plenty of warmth and sunshine to thrive and to flower. On the St John's River, Florida, the plant earned the title: 'the million dollar weed' on account of the way it obstructed navigation. Outside tropical and sub-tropical climates, it is, however, much less prolific. It floats by having a greatly inflated petiole or leaf stalk, which looks like a small green balloon perched on the water. Above the balloon, the stalk narrows and then broadens into a fairly round and curled leaf. The entire plant is a shiny light green. It would be worth growing for that alone, but the flowers are quite superb, a light lilac blue with a spot of yellow, borne on spikes held high above the plant. The bushy, dangling roots, incidentally, make an excellent spawning ground for goldfish. Another plant worth growing for its foliage is the Water Lettuce, *Pistia stratiotes*, which indeed looks rather like a flat lettuce, one that has been gently sat upon. The leaves are a pale shade of green. This is not an easy plant to grow. It requires a temperature in excess of 20°C., and soft water; and it does better in shallow water with its roots within reach of soil. Finally, if you are lucky enough to be able to find them or obtain a few seeds of the Water Chestnut, *Trapa natans* (p. 50), which is a native of Europe naturalized to a limited extent in North America, you can enjoy the fruits raw or roasted. They are sweeter before the shells have hardened. Apart from being edible, the plant is worth growing for its beautiful bronze and green foliage. It is an annual, the fruits rarely ripen in Britain and the plant appears to be growing scarcer on the European continent.

If you happen to live within easy reach of a horticultural establishment which specializes in aquatic plants, do not let your enthusiasm run away with you. Can I make a plea for a stretch of plain water? In every pond, whatever the size, the reflection of waterside plants is one of the finest qualities that water can provide. Too many floating plants and oxygenators breaking the surface will spoil

or destroy that quality. And besides, there should not be so many floating plants on the surface as to detract from the greatest of all aquatic plants: the water lily.

A beautiful woodland pond at Glendalough House excavated in the middle of the last century when it was possible for a well-to-do landowner to call up fifty men for the job. Today the work would be done by machine. The island is an attractive feature and well worth including since there is still plenty of water surface. The scene would, I think, appear far less tranquil if most of the water was given over to water lilies.

53

4

THE
WATER LILY

The number of hardy water lilies, hybrid or otherwise, runs into hundreds, unlike many other genera whose hybrids run into many thousands. The reason for this has less connection with the popularity of ponds than with the notorious difficulty of hybridizing the hardy species. Most of the hardy cultivars are infertile and cross-breeding of the few natural plants has hardly ever produced satisfactory results in any systematic way. The exceptions belong mainly to the work of M. Joseph Bory Latour-Marliac (1830-1911) of Temple-sur-Lot in the south of France. During the 1880's when pond building had become a high Victorian fashion, Marliac developed some method of crossing water lilies. Some of his best hybrids bear the Latinized form of his name, *Marliacea*, or that of his son-in-law, Maurice Laydeker (*Laydekeri*). And without doubt, Marliac's hybrids are among the finest available. Sadly, his techniques died with him. He once said it would take forty years of hard work to re-discover them. So far no one has. And the temperate regions of the world are still waiting for a hardy blue water lily.

Conceivably, we may not have to wait for a pure fluke. For there appears to be a revolution round the corner, not only as regards producing hybrids from water lilies, but from the entire plant kingdom. That revolution would consist of the art or science — really a bit of both — whereby part of the recipe

(DNA) for one plant is spliced with part of the recipe of another. To produce a hardy blue water lily, the object of the exercise would be to obtain the hardiness of, say, *Nymphaea alba* and combine it with the blue of the tender, tropical *Nymphaea caerula*. The problem is to identify and, more difficult, to select out the relevant ingredients for such a recipe. We may also look forward to a hardy lily which will remain open until dusk and perhaps on into the hours of darkness. A floodlit pool on a summer's evening can be a superb sight, but one which has the drawback of water lily blooms which are invariably closed. Only among tropical lilies are there species which will open and flower at night.

Since Marliac's day, a certain amount of confusion has arisen among the names of some hybrids, not usually the very best known, but among some of the pinks in particular. You may find that different nurseries — not to mention botanic gardens, which have been notoriously lax in the proper identification of *Nymphaea* in a way that would be inconceivable with roses — use different names for what is obviously the same hybrid. Doubtless over the years, plants and labels get switched round or misplaced and names get changed. The same problem, which after all is a continuous one, arises with other genera; but what *Nymphaea* for so long lacked was an authority which might look into the question

Nymphaea 'Marliacea Chromatella'

of correct identification of water lily species and cultivars. Fortunately this situation has now changed, and the International Water Lily Society is the official registration body. for *Nymphaea* (see Appendix IV). While the problem of identification persists, it is best to buy water lilies from a single nursery where you have seen the hybrids of your choice, or by reference to the same nursery's catalogue.

A water lily of average vigour can be expected to cover a surface area of about 1 square metre. One might nearly double that figure for the more vigorous varieties and halve it for the smaller and miniature forms. The surface spread will depend not only on the species but also on the depth of water, the richness of the soil and whether or not you are growing your lilies in containers. When given complete freedom as in a natural pond, or in a concrete one with soil spread over the entire base, a water lily is likely to double its surface spread over about three seasons. The usual practice is to lift and divide the plants about every third year, otherwise the lily pads no longer float serenely over the water but clump up together. When buying your plants calculate to cover no more than a half to two thirds of the whole surface area of your pond. There is no reason why you should not cover a smaller area, except one plant placed in the corner of a large pond will look decidedly lonely. But the most common mistake is to have too many plants. The pond then looks cramped and your view of fish and underwater life becomes restricted. Do not underestimate the importance of large areas of water free of any plant or obstruction. A pond without that lacks one of its greatest attributes.

Laying down a layer of soil over the entire base of the pond is an outdated and wasteful practice. Water lilies are now usually grown in plastic pots or baskets. Personally I much prefer a solid-sided pot with no perforations. A solid pot prevents soil leaching out into the

pond, which is inevitable with a perforated basket no matter how carefully you line it with hessian or old rags. The idea behind perforated containers is that the roots of the plant can spread out once the soil in the container is exhausted, but the answer to that is that you should be changing the soil every few years, whatever kind of container you use. There is no question about it, solid pots are less messy to deal with. Most water lilies would require a basket about 30 × 30 × 20 cm. high, while a miniature plant would be satisfied with a container as small as 20 × 20 × 10 cm. I have seen lilies grown in plastic milk bottle crates which are sturdy but too large for comfort. Not for the comfort of the water lily, which will happily fill all available space, but for the comfort and convenience of the pond owner. A lily plus soil and water in a container 30 cm. square is quite heavy enough for anyone of average strength.

Water lilies are rich feeders, and yet I am continually surprised to find how well a plant will do in soil that is no more than 10 cm. deep

LEFT *This lily was started in a plastic bag and is now being transferred to a larger basket. Heavy loam layered with well rotted cow manure and left under cover for six months or more is the ideal growing medium for water lilies. But remember that cow manure that is not well matured is a boon to algae. Many gardeners prefer to use only loam and omit the manure.* ABOVE *Placing the basket and lily in the pond.*

and which has not been renewed in years. Ideally, however, lilies should be grown in rich, heavy loam such as one can obtain from the top spit of pasture. Cow manure that has been well matured under cover for several months can be added at the rate of about one part to three or four of loam — a spade-full to each basket. To prevent the manure fouling the water, it is a good idea to place a final layer of plain soil over the mixture; and a light sprinkling of gravel over that may reduce the amount of mud fish tend to produce by grubbing around in the baskets. Cow manure is optional; it can be omitted or crushed bonemeal can be used instead, but never add horse or hen manure which will pollute the water.

Hardy water lilies belong to two genera: *Nymphaea* and *Nuphar*. Unless you happen to have a stretch of water 1.8 metres in depth or

more, or the water in your pond is very acid, then Nuphars are hardly worth growing. They will succeed under both these conditions whereas Nymphaeas will not. The common *Nuphar lutea*, known as the 'Brandy Bottle' on account of its faintly alcoholic smell, is to be found in many European canals, natural ponds and waterways. It has small and round yellow flowers, insignificant compared with any of the Nymphaeas. The North American *Nuphar advena* has slightly larger flowers which, like *lutea*, rise well clear of the surface. But since the leaves are always produced in abundance and measure about 30 cm. long, the flowers, which are only about 7 cm. across, are not very conspicuous. If, however, you do want to grow a *Nuphar* in a small pond, then choose the little *Nuphar pumila (minima)* which flowers freely, has very small leaves and is nothing like as vigorous as the other two.

The rootstocks or rhizomes of Nymphaeas are of two kinds: those which grow horizontally and those which tend to grow vertically or almost so. From the angle at which the

Nuphar lutea – Brandy Bottle

leaves are emerging from the rootstock, it should be possible for you to judge which kind of plant you have. If in doubt, simply make sure that the crown of the plant is above the level of the soil when you plant it. Perhaps more water lilies fail by being completely buried than for any other reason. The best time for obtaining plants is in late spring after growth is well under way. Water lilies should not be moved before growth has started nor, for that matter, after growth has ceased in autumn. A young lily plant will be given the best possible chance if it is started in shallow water. Either place your plant and basket on a series of bricks and keep removing bricks to lower the plant as it gains in vigour, or start with the pond only partially filled and gradually top it up. When you buy a water lily you may get a tuber which has been cut off a parent rootstock. After a few seasons your young tuber will have matured and developed several offspring of its own. It is a simple matter to slice through the tubers, and the divided rootstocks can be replanted. If you want to propagate a large number of plants , lift the tuber and examine it for 'eyes'. These are small, immature buds, no more than little bulges, not unlike large warts with tiny leaves, growing on the tuber. These can be gouged out with a sharp knife, leaving a little of the main tuber on the 'eye'. Prepare a shallow tray of equal parts of sharp sand and loam, and a little crushed charcoal can be added to keep the soil sweet. Plant the 'eyes' in the tray, making sure that their crowns are exposed, and place the tray in very shallow water — 2-3 cm. is quite deep enough to start the eyes. Fish and stray bits of oxygenating plants should be kept well away from the tray. And a piece of net wire placed over the tray may discourage birds from rooting around in it and, as sometimes happens, pulling up the baby tubers. As leaves develop, gradually increase the depth of water over the plants. Replanting of the tubers into

separate baskets can take place as soon as they each have a number of well-developed leaves.

Water lilies are adaptable plants, but they should be chosen not only for their shape and colour but for the depth of water to which they are best suited. The most vigorous plants will thrive in depths of 0.75 to 1 metre and more. Plants of medium vigour are normally grown in depths ranging from 45 to 60 cm., while the small and miniature plants need no

The pads or leaves of water lilies tend to heap up on each other, if the tubers are not thinned out from time to time, ideally about every three years.

BELOW RIGHT *A mature tuber. The long, white hairless roots are anchor roots and can be cut off before replanting the tuber, if desired. Roots with 'hairs' are those which provide the plant with nutrition and should be left intact.*

BELOW *A fairly well developed lily 'eye' or nodule. If gouged out this eye would quickly develop into a mature plant.*

BOTTOM *The tuber of a mature water lily such as 'Gladstoniana' would be as thick as your arm. By comparison this young tuber of the miniature Nymphaea helvola is smaller than a thumb.*

more than 20-30 cm. of water above their crowns. This, at least, is how commercial growers usually classify their plants. But, with the exception of the miniature water lilies, one could certainly add at least another 25 cm. to the depth in each case and that would be, in my opinion, an advantage. You may wonder what happens if a lily is placed in a depth of water other than recommended. In water that is too deep, a plant may not have the stamina to send leaves to the surface and so it will eventually die; or it may survive but flower only occasionally or not at all. On the other hand, in water that is too shallow, the flowers will be small and not necessarily more numerous, the leaves will not be able to spread out properly and will quickly heap up

on each other. Shallow water does have one advantage, however. It will warm up earlier in the season and the plants will develop and flower earlier. This might be worth bearing in mind if you live in northerly latitudes, Scotland or Norway for instance, which have short growing seasons, or if for some reason your pond is not exposed to direct sunlight throughout the day. Otherwise I recommend growing water lilies in water which at least approaches the maximum rather than the minimum depth. The blooms will be larger, and the leaves, well spread out, will give the plant a much finer appearance.

If you have a large, deep pond or a lake and you want a white water lily, then *Nymphaea* 'Gladstoniana' might well be your first choice. Under ideal conditions this very vigorous plant can produce massive white flowers 20 cm. across and more. It should be grown only in very deep water — 1.3 metres is not too deep — as it produces a great number of leaves. Slightly smaller and less vigorous, but no less beautiful, is the native European water lily, *Nymphaea alba*. Many a wild lake is given a touch of serenity by the lovely white flowers of this plant. It will grow in slow moving rivers and is sometimes to be found in water as much as 3 metres deep. For the more moderate water scheme N. 'Marliacea Albida' is an excellent choice as it is a very prolific bloomer. Double flowers are not at all common among water lilies, but Marliac's 'Gloire de Temple-sur-Lot' produces magnificent flowers, each containing a profusion of petals which makes this plant, unmistakably, a true double. The petals, at first, are tinged with pink and clear to white the day after the flowers open. 'Temple-sur-Lot' may take a few seasons before reaching its full blooming capacity. 'Gonnère' is another double, without quite the same density of petals, but a good choice, nevertheless, for the medium to deep pond. The North American *Nymphaea odorata* is a vigorous white water lily suitable for ponds of medium depth, while the less vigorous 'Albatross' is better suited to the smaller pond. And if you have only a tiny tub pond or a sink, then choose the smallest white lily of all, N. *pygmaea alba* which has flowers 3.5 cm. across and needs only a few centimetres of water over its crown.

Nymphaea Mme. 'Wilfron Gonnère'

Most pond owners will want to grow more than one lily. To obtain the maximum contrast with a white lily one should choose a red variety. By general consent the most outstanding red available is *Nymphaea* 'Escarboucle'. It produces large, deep crimson flowers which are probably the most conspicuous of any water lily. 'Escarboucle', you may find, throws up red flowers blotched with white during its first season. The following year, however, the flowers will be perfectly red. The same sometimes applies to the offshoots.

This picture gives a good idea of just how small are the flowers of the miniature and dwarf hardy Nymphaea, in this instance a Laydekeri hybrid. Miniature forms are very useful for small ponds and tub ponds.

Do not think that your plant has some ailment, it is simply a characteristic of 'Escarboucle'. Medium to deep ponds are best suited to this lily. At the other end of the scale, for shallow ponds, *N.* 'Froebeli' (p.63) surely ranks as one of the best reds. In colour it is not unlike 'Escarboucle' since it has deep wine-red flowers. These rise well above the surface of the water and are produced in abundance. 'Froebeli' will flower well into the autumn, and I fancy will remain open in colder weather than most. In vigour mid-way between 'Escarboucle' and 'Froebeli' is *N.* 'Laydekeri Purpurata', another plant with rich red flowers and very free-blooming. Somewhat larger, though still in the small category, is *N.* 'Fulgens', which has flowers of the most brilliant red produced in large numbers. If you are attracted to having both red and white in the same flower, then grow 'Attraction' which is of medium vigour and which produces garnet red flowers tipped with white. For deep water, there is 'Conqueror' whose flowers become a darker red from the centre outwards and are flecked with white. And for the large pond, one might well choose the magnificent 'Charles de Meurville' which sends up massive red flowers, but which needs plenty of space. More adaptable as regards depth is 'Gloriosa', whose blooms darken with age from carmine to deep rose. This is a plant which will thrive in water of medium depth but it will also do well in deeper water if necessary.

Sometimes described as a red lily is 'James Brydon' (p.63). Rich pink is, I think, a better description. This American lily is arguably the best choice of all to make if one were limited to a single specimen. In the first place the number of flowers the plant produces in relation to the number of leaves is high. The plant will continue to flower even when cloudy weather or reduction in sunshine prevents most others flowering. And the flowers of 'James Brydon' are very beautiful.

62

The water lily

LEFT *Nymphaea 'Fulgens' not only produces blooms of bright red but produces them in quantity.*

RIGHT *N. 'Indiana' is a small variety which produces flowers which change colour with age, as this picture illustrates. The dark red colour is achieved on about the third day of opening.*

BELOW *N. 'Froebeli' is regarded as one of the most reliable of the smaller varieties, producing flowers consistently right through the season.*

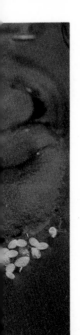

FAR LEFT *Nymphaea 'Escarboucle', and* LEFT *Nymphaea 'Helvola', a miniature form with starry yellow blooms and spotted foliage. It is an excellent choice for the small pond, producing an abundance of flowers right through the summer.*

Cup-shaped, exquisitely formed, with an even distribution of this rich pink hue — unobtainable in any other water lily — it has vivid golden stamens which are well set off by this pink cup. And finally, 'James Brydon' makes a good cut flower. It requires a pool of shallow to medium depth. If this lily has a drawback, it lies, I think, in the very definiteness of that pink. Something more delicate is obtainable in the muted, blush pink of a 'Marliacea Carnea' or the denser pink of 'Marliacea Rosea'. Both plants have dark green leaves and are of medium vigour. For the larger, deeper pond 'Colossea', another blush pink and a prolific plant, would be a

63

good choice. A double pink is to be had in 'Mme Wilfron Gonnère, not to be confused with the double white, 'Gonnère'. For star-shaped flowers held high above the surface, choose *N. odorata* 'W. B. Shaw' which is suitable for shallow to medium depths. So also is *N. tuberosa rosea*, which produces soft pink flowers, and like 'W. B. Shaw' is usually described as fragrant. But one normally has to approach a lily bloom closely before the fragrance is apparent; hardy water lilies will not fill the air with sweet scent in the manner of a honeysuckle. For the smaller pond, 'Laydekeri lilacea' is a good choice, requiring only a limited amount of space. It has flowers that vary in colour from soft to deep rose. In the same bracket is 'Rose Arey', notable for its incurving petals.

If one is limited to two plants, I am inclined to think that a combination of a yellow with a white lily is preferable to either coupled with red. Red and pink are more dominant colours which demand attention. A soft yellow has a quiet grace which one may feel is more in keeping with the restful, soothing ambiance that one expects of a small garden pond. With this in mind, one could hardly do better than choose the almost impalpable yellow of 'Marliacea Chromatella'. This lovely plant is well suited to medium to deep ponds. The smaller, less vigorous 'Moorei' has flowers of a slightly darker yellow. Otherwise the plants are almost identical, their leaves being dark green, heavily blotched or spotted with purple. The large yellow flowers of 'Sunrise' make it a popular plant, especially as it is adaptable, vigorous in deep water but not uncontrollable in shallower depths. 'Colonel A.J. Walsh' is certainly a vigorous plant producing canary yellow blooms high above the water. It does tend however, to look rather unwieldy. Another plant which holds its blooms high is *N. odorata* 'Sulphurea Grandiflora'. It is nothing like so vigorous as 'Colonel A.J. Walsh', so it should be grown in about 50 cm. of water.

Nymphaea 'Sunrise'

And a miniature yellow is available in *N. pygmaea* 'Helvola', a prolific little plant with finely marked leaves. There are also a number of water lilies whose flowers tend to change in colour as they age. The flowers of 'Indiana', for example, open a shade of orange-red and then deepen to a coppery red. 'Paul Hariot' has blooms which begin a pale yellow and change to shades of red, while 'Sioux' has yellow flowers which darken to peach. All the plants are on the small side and will do best with about 45 cm. of water over their crowns.

These plants are representative of any selection of water lilies held by commercial growers. There are many more plants from which to choose and there is no substitute for actually seeing any particular species in bloom. But I would stress the importance of matching your choice of plant with the depth of your pond. This way you will get the best results from your water lily. Resist the temptation to fall in love with a plant whose needs are not met by your particular pond.

In America, cross-breeding of tropical water-lilies has produced many spectacular results. Unlike the hardy varieties, tropical lilies and their hybrids are often extremely fertile and this has given rise to many hundreds of cultivars. Sadly, their brilliant colours and often superb fragrance are the prerogatives of warm climates. In some Mediterranean areas it is possible to grow tropical water lilies outdoors in summer and to keep the tubers in damp sand (young tubers or eyes have the best chance of surviving) during the winter. Alternatively, the plant can be treated as an annual, new stock being bought each spring, or you may succeed in raising the plant from seed. Few tropical lilies will grow well in water which is below 21°C. So it is difficult to obtain consistent results in Britian and indeed in much of Europe. A conservatory pool, perhaps with the addition of artificial heat, may be the only answer. But if you live in an

Tropical water lily, Nymphaea colorata.

area with a consistently high summer temperature, then tender lilies can be started into growth in a glass house in early spring and placed in the outdoor pool later. When the leaves die back towards the end of summer, that is the time to lift the plant and attempt to winter it in damp sand, well away from rodents, incidentally, which are partial to lily tubers. Free circulation of air is important too during storage, so cover whatever container you use with wire mesh but do not seal it. A comparatively cool temperature is best during storage: 10—15°C. Tropical lilies are rich feeders and need plenty of space but little water over the crown. A half-and-half mixture of well rotted cow manure and loam is ideal. Temperature apart, tender water lilies are no more difficult to grow than hardy ones. Among day-blooming tropical lilies, the pale bluey pink *Nymphaea stellata* stands a good chance of blooming in less than the best conditions. And *Nymphaea caerula*, another light blue, may remain open after dark

LEFT *The Tropical Nymphaea 'Panama Pacific',* and BELOW *Nymphaea stellata cyanea.*

66

ABOVE *Tropical Nymphaea 'Red Flare', and* RIGHT *the night-blooming tropical 'Mrs George Hitchcock'.*

if the temperature remains sufficiently high. *N.* 'Pamela' with flowers of the palest blue can do well in less than ideal conditions. Another obliging tropical is *N.* 'Director Moore' which contrasts well with 'Pamela', having flowers of very rich, purplish blue. If low light values is a problem for you, then you could try these water lilies, or *N.* 'Daubeniana' (another light blue variety) or 'Pink Platter', as these will produce flowers with less sunshine than most other tropicals. But for water gardeners who live in the tropics or in areas with long, hot, brilliant summer days and warm nights, the range of tropical *Nymphaea* is one of abundance; and if space permits, the inclusion of a few tropicals in your pond should provide vivid flowers in contrasting colours all summer long. Among the white varieties, *N*. 'Marian Strawn' is a prolific day bloomer, as is *N*. 'Mrs George H. Pring'; while *N*. 'Aviator Pring' and *N*. 'St Louis' are among the most popular yellow varieties. Among the pinks, 'General Pershing', a variety which dates form 1917, remains among the best known tropicals. 'Evelyn Randig' has pink flowers of a darker hue, and the blooms are held well above the surface of the water — a characteristic of tropicals, though few rise so high or so consistently as this variety. In addition, some growers enjoy the purplish brown markings on the leaves of 'Evelyn Randig', which are somewhat more emphatic than with most other blotched varieties. A curiosity among water lilies, and a most attractive one, is a hybrid known as 'Green Smoke'. The name is apt, for the petals are bluish at the tips and a shade of soft green thereafter.

One of the greatest delights of the water garden in warm climates are the night-blooming *Nymphaea*. The temperate zones have nothing to equal the fragrance of large blooms held high over still water on balmy nights. Night-blooming tropicals make good

cut flowers, and I shall not easily forget the first occasion when I stayed in a house filled with these exotic and opulent blooms; their heady scent, like no other flower I know, remains a remembered pleasure. At Longwood Gardens, Kennet Square, Pennsylvania, the night-blooming tropicals are picked out, highlighted by individual spotlights attached to heavy but movable bases in the ponds, so that the lights can be shifted as required. If you have the opportunity to grow these splendid plants, some form of lighting, especially if you have your pond on a patio, can add significantly to the pleasure of a water garden. Not only are evenings the period when most people have the best opportunity of enjoying their garden, but it is striking how different a floodlit garden is from its daylight counterpart. It is almost like visiting two different places. And night-blooming tropicals enliven water in darkness as no other plant can. The brilliance of 'Emily Grant Hutchings' or 'H.C. Haarstick' when floodlit is sufficient reason in itself for having a pond. Both varieties have flowers of the richest pink, while 'Mrs George C. Hitchcock' has pink petals with a touch of white running through the centres. All are prolific bloomers. *N*. 'Red Flare' has petals of the deepest pure red and stamens that are maroon. For contrast you could choose from the splendid white varieties, which include 'Missouri' with its exceptionally large flowers, sometimes 60 cm. and more across, and which live longer than most; and 'Juno', an adaptable variety which will thrive in deep or shallow water.

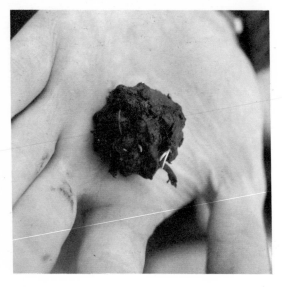

LEFT *Tropical lily tuber. It is easy to break off the emerging shoot, so care should be taken when planting.*

TOP RIGHT *An indoor tropical pool showing the heating system. The large, deep pit in the middle is used for planting the Victoria lily (Victoria amazonica), a hungry feeder. Tropical Nymphaea are grown in baskets around the pool. Note how shallow the pool is (about 45 cm. deep) compared with ponds designed to grow temperate lilies.* BELOW RIGHT *The massive Victoria amazonica in flower in the same pool. (National Botanic Gardens, Dublin).*

Nelumbo 'Mono botan'

What goes for the tender water lilies goes also for the *Nelumbo (Nelumbium)* or Lotus, except the lotus requires a longer growing season in order to survive and will not set seed easily. Plants will not necessarily succumb to cold. In fact *Nelumbo* is fairly hardy, although it should be protected from frost. It is because in northerly climates the growing season is short that *Nelumbo* may fail, the tubers becoming weak through undernourishment. The tubers should be planted horizontally, or the lotus can be propagated from nodes taken from the extensive runners which may reach 7 or 10 metres in length in a single season. This is a good reason for growing Nelumbos in round containers, as there is less chance of the runners bunching up as they always do at the corner of square containers. Nodes taken from runners must be kept moist and warm. In America, a native form thrives particularly in the central states and around the Great Lakes. In Southern Europe the lotus does well, and open-air cultivation is certainly possible within the vine-growing districts — and as far north as Vienna. But so far as Britain is concerned, it is really a conservatory or hot house plant, not one for the outdoor pond. Their broad, stately leaves and height — they can be as tall as a man — means they are superbly ornamental, particularly perhaps when grown in large tubs around a patio. This might be one way of growing them in the open in Britain for a month or two, if you can conceive of a means of transporting a heavy tub from a hot house to the patio and back.

The lotus has a magnificent flower not unlike a paeony. The American lotus, *Nelumbo lutea*, has pale, sulphur yellow flowers which can be as much as 25 cm. across. The Indian lotus, *Nelumbo nucifera* (facing) is the species most people probably think of as 'the lotus'. It has vivid pink flowers, sometimes larger even than *N. lutea*, and is an exceptionally vigorous species. In the wild it is not unusual to see this lotus covering many acres of shallow water.

There are many fine cultivars including double and dwarf forms. Among the largest is N. 'alba grandiflora', the flowers of which are not only enormous but fragrant too. A hybrid which has flowers with two colours is *N. nucifera* 'Empress'; the petals are basically white but the edges are touched with crimson. It is a striking form. If you want a lotus with pure red flowers such is available with *N. n.* 'Red Lotus' — rich rose is how the flowers might be described. Double forms are represented by N. 'Roseum Plenum', which has pink flowers, and N. 'Shiroman', which has very double, cream-coloured flowers that become pure white with age. Another cultivar with flowers that change colour is N. 'Mrs Perry D. Slocum'. The flowers open pink and turn yellow, so that you can have blooms of quite different colours on the one plant.

If space is limited you should try the miniature lotus that grows to no great height, requires less root space, but still produces flowers of perfect shape and superb colour. The Tulip Lotus *N. nucifera* 'Shirokunshi' has creamy white flowers and grows only about 45 cm. tall. Of similar height is 'Mono Botan'

Nelumbo nucifera or lotus. The vivid pink blooms of lotus are initially globular and then the petals peel back, as in the picture, to reveal fully the brilliant yellow (sometimes reddish) centre.

which has very double flowers of vivid pink; and there is even a dwarf form known as 'Mono Botan minima' which may reach a height of only 40 cm., sometimes less. So although the larger forms of lotus do require reasonable space, a dwarf lotus can be accommodated in a small pool, and few aquatic plants are more graceful or lovely.

Before turning our attention to marginal plants, mention should be made of a number of other plants which may be grown in deep or shallow water, have floating leaves and very worthwhile flowers. They are species which complement water lilies, being smaller and daintier. Water Fringe (called variously *Villarsia nymphoides, Nymphoides peltata, Limnathemum peltatum* and *L. nymphoides*) has heart-shaped leaves very similar to water lily pads, but much smaller. They are only about 5 cm. across, crinkled at the edges and mottled with

The little Water Fringe, Villarsia nymphoides. The flower is only slightly larger than the area enclosed by a thumb and forefinger.

ABOVE *The flower and leaf of the Water Hawthorn Aponogeton distachyus. You will extend the flowering season within your pond by including this fine plant.*

BELOW *The four-leaf water clover, Marsilia mutica.*

purple. A plain-leafed version is known as *N.* 'Bennetii'. In late summer, the Water Fringe bears little yellow trumpet flowers held a few centimetres above the surface. The individual blooms do not last long, but a plant can bear a fair number over a long period. Despite its name, Water Fringe is as happy in 60 or 90 cm. of water as it is in a shallow pool. In fact, it is a rampant plant and needs to be controlled. *Nymphoides* is also represented among tender aquatics, and what is quaintly called White Snowflake, *N. cristatum*, will produce a mass of pretty white flowers in tropical and sub-tropical conditions. There is also a Yellow Snowflake, *N. geminata*. Both can be grown in water that is very shallow, a few centimetres deep or up to 30 cm.

Likewise the Water Poppy, *Hydrocleys nymphoides*, which also has yellow flowers: very bright they are too, and produced in great abundance. They are three-petalled and cup-shaped. Even if you do not live in the sub-tropics, you may be able to overwinter the Water Poppy outdoors if the weather remains mild. Though it does not bear flowers, the Four Leaf Water Clover, *Marsilia mutica*, is grown for its ornamental leaves; not only is the shape of the leaf unusual, so too is the patterning on each leaf. Beginning with a yellow centre, it forms a clover shape in light green before repeating the pattern in a darker shade. Another deep water aquatic, hardy this time, deserves a brief description. Sometimes it is difficult to transplant, but it is a popular species and is found in many ornamental ponds. It is the Water Hawthorn or *Aponogeton distachyus*, which has long strap-like leaves of dark green or, occasionally, brown. It bears soft white flowers with anthers which are conspicuous by being jet black. In frost-free ponds Water Hawthorn will continue to flower well into the winter months. It is not unusual to see it in flower at Christmas and indeed in January and February.

5 MARGINAL PLANTS FOR THE POOL

If you are fortunate enough to live in the country or enjoy tramping across the countryside around lakes and natural ponds and rivers, you can hardly have failed to notice how plants grow in their natural habitats. Frequently a number of species will grow in profusion together, inter-mixed in a haphazard fashion. But you will also see, especially if you follow a river for any distance, that at one spot a particular plant flourishes only to disappear completely round the next bend where another kind has taken hold. This in its turn vanishes and on the far bank a third plant has colonized, and so on. And so it should be in a pond. In a confined space, plants which are mixed together only create a confused vision. Similarly, one specimen of ten plants, planted one after the other, will present a scheme lacking in character. What one should aim for is a mass of one plant followed by a showy mass of another. Almost all marginal plants are easily propagated by division, so even if you obtain only one specimen initially, within a season or two you can easily achieve the right effect. Firm, definite groupings of a few plants is very much more desirable than a hotch-potch of many.

Marginal plants, for want of a definition, are those which grow in shallow water or in soil that is saturated in water. They have a flowering period which ranges from early spring until autumn. One plant precedes all. That is the lovely *Caltha palustris*, often called Marsh Marigold or Kingcup. I do not think there is any other waterside plant that has given me more pleasure. There comes one of those early spring days when the breeze carries the heady smell of new growth. A new warmth pervades the air and there on the edge of the pool the Marsh Marigold has opened her brilliant yellow flowers. The quality of that yellow seems to me unequalled. I can picture now, in my mind's eye, spring evenings when the sun has just passed over the pond and the flower of the Marsh Marigold seems almost luminous against the dank brown that still remains of last year's growth. The Marsh Marigold produces a mass of flowers that will remain in flower for several weeks. (I also grow the lilac-flowering *Rhododendron* 'Praecox' and masses of the early *Erica* 'Springwood White', so that new life around the pool begins not long after the New Year.) The Marsh Marigold abounds throughout Europe and parts of North America. It reaches a height of about 30 cm., grows best in moist soil or very shallow water and is easily propagated by seed or division. A double variety, *Caltha palustris flore pleno*, is slightly smaller and less vigorous, but it can produce such a wealth of flowers as to almost conceal the plant beneath them. An altogether larger version is avail-

able in *Caltha polypetala* which grows up to 60 or 90 cm. And from the Himalayas comes a small white version, *Caltha palustris alba,* which may grow no more than 15 or 20 cm. high. These are all excellent plants for concealing an unsightly piece of concrete margin. In shallow water, their generally bushy habit will obscure the margin behind, while planted around the pool, some of the leaves will tend, conveniently, to flop informally over the edge of the bank.

Equally suitable for hiding a few metres of ugly margin is the Bog Bean, or *Menyanthes trifoliata* (p.103), so called because its light green leaves are divided into three well-defined parts. Growing about 30 cm. high, the Bog Bean has a horizontal rootstock and enjoys stretching across the surface of the water

LEFT AND BELOW *Single and double flowers of the Marsh Marigold, Caltha palustris.*

The Great Water Plantain in a lakeside setting

rather like a floating plant. And even if you have no margin that needs concealing, the Bog Bean is well worth growing for its unique flowers. They come just about the time the Marsh Marigold is on the wane or is over. Conspicuous rich pink buds peel back to reveal five snowy white petals which are crested on their surface with long, curly white hairs and these give the flower a fluffy or even a frosty appearance. This is certainly a flower worth examining closely. Look at how snugly the stamens fit around the base of the petals, each with their bright yellow pollen load, and how the light green style protrudes just above the level of the curling hairs. There is no daintier flower among the marginals; a watchmaker might baulk at constructing anything so delicate. Common to many boglands throughout Europe, Asia and North America, *Menyanthes trifoliata* is a plant of vigorous growth but one that can be cut back easily.

Brass Buttons, or *Cotula coronopifolia*, is another plant that enjoys scrambling about the margin in shallow water. The flower consists of a small disc of matt yellow, in itself not very exciting, but where there are tens of these flowers appearing together, as they do during the summer, the effect is lovely. The flowers bend over slightly on top of their thin, elegant stems, looking like so many miniature periscopes. The plant is unlikely to exceed 25 cm. in height. In winter it may die back altogether, as an annual, in which case you are dependent upon the seeds. So do not renew the soil in the basket or around the margin until the new plants have come up the following spring. In the Southern Hemisphere, in South Africa and Australia, where *Cotula coronopifolia* is a native, it can tend to be rather invasive. In more temperate zones it can be introduced safely.

The same cannot be said about the Great Water Plantain, *Alisma plantago-aquatica*, a plant common throughout parts of the Northern Hemisphere. Grown in moist soil or shallow

75

water, it is far from fussy. It throws up ellip-
tic, erect leaves on long stalks, reaching a
height of anything from 30 to 90 cm. In mid to
late summer appear the tiny nondescript pink
or white flowers. What makes the plant so
attractive is the pyramidal panicle upon which
the flowers appear. Less attractive is the
Water Plantain's habit of setting seed anywhere and everywhere. If you introduced this
plant then be sure to cut out the panicles as
soon as the flowers are over. A more suitable
form, because less rampant, is *Alisma lanceola-
tum* which has long slender leaves and height
of about 30-40 cm. But it is also rarer and you
may not find it easy to obtain.

No such problem should arise with the popular little Bog Arum, *Calla palustris,* and since it
grows no more than 25 cm. in height and is
compact in habit it is an obvious choice for the
small pool. It thrives with 5 cm. of water over
its crown and produces a small white trumpet
flower in summer. Comes the autumn and
the flowers have been replaced by fruits of
brilliant scarlet. A more familiar arum is
Zantedeschia aethiopica (also known as *Calla aethiopica* and *Richardia africana*) or Arum Lily which
grows to a height of 60 to 90 cm. and bears
magnificent trumpet flowers of pure white
with a yellow 'poker' or spadix within. This
plant is not really hardy however, and
should be wintered in a cold house which is
frost-free. Alternatively, if you experience
only mild frosts, the Arum Lily should survive in the pool the whole year round if it has
20 or 30 cm. of water above its crown. Another plant with white trumpet-shaped flowers
is to be had in *Lysichitum camtschatcense*. Whether
it be planted in moist soil or shallow water
this plant does require deep soil: 50 cm. is not

Arum lilies along a river bank

too much. Once established it is a difficult plant to lift intact. Raising the plant from seed is rather easier though several years must elapse before the young plants can be expected to flower. The leaves, which vary from 30 to 100 cm. in length, arise almost stemless from the base of the plant. Even when the plant does not attain its maximum height, I find its broad leaves rather too bulky in appearance for a small, compact pool. It looks best when one has plenty of space and other shrubby plants with which it can harmonize. This applies even more to the somewhat taller and broader *Lysichitum americanum* or False American Skunk Cabbage. However, where space permits, this plant produces a welcome contrast to *camtschatcense* and indeed *Calla palustris* in bearing yellow trumpets.

White and yellow are common colours among marginal flowers, whereas blue is comparatively rare. The prostate and rambling *Veronica beccabunga* or Brooklime produces small blue flowers on racemes in the leaf axils. Grow the plant if you would like to try the leaves as a spring salad, but it has to be said that so far as the flowers are concerned they are rather dull and inconspicuous. A much more brilliant blue is to be had in the Water-Forget-Me-Not or *Myosotis scorpioides (palustris)* and especially in the improved 'Mermaid' strain. The plant varies very much in height, but 20 cm. would be about average; it flowers profusely over a long period and sets seed easily, so that you should have a fine mass of this showy little marginal in a matter of a few seasons. And it thrives in shade. Quite a few plants have been called Forget-Me-Nots from time to time, but the water plant has the greatest claim to the name on account of being named such by German botanists way back in the Middle Ages. But there are more romantic accounts of how the *Myosotis* received its name. One such legend, from the sixteenth century, tells the story of a knight who was taking a stroll with his lady-love along the banks of the

LEFT *The Bog Arum – Calla palustris.* BELOW *Veronica beccabunga or Brooklime.*

River Danube on the eve of their wedding. The lady, to her distress, spotted a spray of these flowers being carried away by the river. Instantly the knight plunged into the river to retrieve them. He reached the flowers only to find that the current was too strong for him to return to the shore. As he was swept by his lady-love he threw the fatal flowers on to the bank beside her, with the exclamation: *'Vergiss mich nicht!'* — 'Forget-me-not!' It is said too that youths in medieval times garlanded their

Lysichitum americanum

Water Mint has a whorl of soft lilac-blue flowers.

loved ones with chains of Forget-Me-Nots.

The plant is small enough for the smallest pond and conspicuous enough for the largest. For the same reason Water Mint or *Mentha aquatica* should have a place in any water scheme. It will grow in damp soil or under several centimetres of water. The leaves are rather hairy and are found in two colours, a dark maroon colour and a bright green. In the wild, it is commonly found in wetlands adjacent to rivers and lakes, and you will often find plants with both these colours living within a few metres of each other, and sometimes both colours on the one plant. A keen observer will easily discover why. In shade, where the plant does well, the leaves remain green, but when exposed to sunlight for any length of time they soon turn to a purplish maroon hue. Under very favourable conditions Water Mint can reach a height in excess of a metre. But in a confined space the likely

BELOW AND RIGHT *Flower and leaf of the Pickerel Weed,*
Pontederia cordata.

height is about 30 cm. Keep a sufficient number of the plants from which to pluck off leaves to flavour your potatoes. And enjoy the bright whorls of lilac-blue flowers that appear at the end of the summer.

Blue flowers are also produced by the Pickerel Weed or *Pontederia cordata,* some say the best blue flowers of all water plants. But the flowers apart, this is a handsome plant by any standards, sending up light green cordate or heart-shaped leaves on long stalks, and rising 45-75 cm. above water level. It does best in water no more than 12 cm. above its crown, and towards the end of summer the flowers appear on spikes. Not all the flowers on any one spike will necessarily open at the one time, which can give the spike a slightly moth-eaten appearance, it seems to me. But when the Pickerel Weed is grown in sufficient numbers, the individual spikes give way to a mass effect of medium blue. *Pontederia lanceolata* has, as the name suggests, rather more lance-shaped leaves and it grows very much larger, often to 1.5 metres in height, but this species is not fully hardy.

Even more dramatic than the lance-shaped leaves of the *Pontederia* are the arrowhead-shaped leaves of *Sagittaria sagittifolia.* The plant, also known as Common Arrowhead, is best stood in 10-15 cm. of water but it will often thrive in greater depths. The roots need confining as they are stoloniferous and spread

79

LEFT *Sagittaria sagittifolia, Common Arrowhead.* BELOW LEFT *Japanese Arrowhead, Sagittaria japonica flore pleno.*

rapidly. Occasionally some of the leaves may float on the water, but generally they rise, more or less perpendicularly, 40 cm. above the water surface. The white flowers are produced in midsummer. A larger variety comes in *Sagittaria japonica,* but the one to obtain, if at all possible, is the double form, *Sagittaria japonica flore pleno,* which grows to much the same size as the Common Arrowhead but much more slowly, and there is no need to contain the roots. And the flowers are so double as to seem almost like small snowballs. For effective foliage and flowers this plant should rank high on any choice list of water plants.

Effective foliage is a good reason for growing *Ranunculus lingua* (especially the larger *grandiflora* form), which often reaches a metre in height. Green sword-shaped leaves come off a broad stem knuckled like bamboo and flushed with a hue of dark pink. Ranunculus comes from the Latin name for frog, *Rana,* an allusion to the fact that many of the species inhabit wet places. As the common name of the plant, Tongue Buttercup, implies, it produces flowers very like the common buttercup of the meadow that we all picked as children, only in the *grandiflora* form, they are somewhat larger — often exceeding 5 cm. across. The plant can be expected to flower throughout the summer and even into the autumn. On account of its rather thin flower stems, however, the plant can look rather gangly and

The Branched Bur Reed, Sparganium erectum. This photograph well illustrates its fine structure. The large burs are the female flowers, the smaller ones above are the male ones.

Some gardeners feel the Bur Reed or *Sparganium erectum* is not a plant worth including in the garden. True, its strap-like leaves which rise from the base in two distinct ranks are not of great interest and the flowers are not colourful. Nevertheless, the flowers, the large female burs and the smaller male ones, do create an unusual design unlike any other plant. So if you have a keen eye for structure this is a plant you might care to grow. It is quite happy to stand in water of any depth up to 45 cm., a useful feature since few other plants will tolerate that depth. However, if you have but one bay of that depth, then the

windswept after stormy weather. If you have a sheltered corner, place it there in shallow water, and contain the stoloniferous roots which can send up shoots at a considerable distance from the parent plant.

Less susceptible to wind is *Butomus umbellatus* or Flowering Rush. It grows to much the same height as the Tongue Buttercup, around a metre, and thrives in water up to 10 cm. deep. The long, thin leaves are shaped rather like stilettoes and are occasionally twisted. In midsummer come the flowers, sometimes light pink, sometimes almost maroon. Rising from their stalks, the whole flower head resembles the structure of an inverted umbrella, hence the name *umbellatus*. A single umbel may produce as many as thirty flowers. The plant is found in Europe and Asia, and its colourfulness and shape make it an obvious choice for the garden pond.

BELOW *Planting a fine specimen of the Tongue Buttercup, Ranunculus lingua grandiflora. A pot would be better than a basket.*

RIGHT *An informal pond combined with a rockery. The rocks have been skilfully set in mortar with planting spaces left at random points. By this means maintenance of the rockery is minimised.*

LEFT *The flower head of the Water Gladiole, Butomus umbellatus.*

BELOW *The Golden Club, Orontium aquaticum in flower.*

Bur Reed should hardly be your first choice.

That distinction should surely go to the Golden Club, *Orontium aquaticum*, a versatile and highly spectacular plant. The leaves are of a dark velvety green on their upper side and of a silvery sheen underneath. When planted in deep water the leaves tend to float, whereas in moist soil at the pond's edge — where the plant will do equally well — the leaves grow more or less upright to a height of about 45 cm. Then, of course, the contrasting shades of the leaves can be appreciated to the full, especially when a light breeze creates a shimmering effect. In spring and early summer, the Golden Club produces a large number of strikingly white stems or spadices, at the ends

83

Typha latifolia

of which appear the bright yellow flowers. The effect is of a brilliant white matchstick with a yellow head. Matchsticks however, do not come 30 cm. long and as thick as your finger. So it is both the size and colour of the flowers as well as the leaves which make the Golden Club so fine a waterside plant. It does have the disadvantage of requiring deep soil, 45 cm. at least, and once established the plant can only be lifted with difficulty. Propagate by seed, starting them in shallow water.

Everyone who owns a pond will want to grow *Typha,* and with good reason. The long rush-like leaves and the tall brown pokers of the Reed Mace or Bulrush as *Typha* is commonly called, are for most people inseparable from water. The question is which *Typha* to grow. The commonly found *Typha latifolia* is a magnificent plant, but one which can produce a veritable forest of vegetation two or more metres in height. Clearly this is only a plant for lakes and very large water schemes. The more slender *Typha angustifolia* can reach a similar height, but will remain somewhat shorter if kept within bounds and it should still flower reasonably well. In the wild, the two plants can be distinguished by the fact that the leaves of *Typha latifolia* are mostly 1 cm. or more in width, while those of *Typha angustifolia* do not usually exceed 0.5 cm. Shorter species of Reed Mace, namely *Typha Shuttleworthii* and *Laxmanii* are perhaps more suited to the garden pool, but these plants are not so easy to come by. So, for most gardeners, the best choice is *Typha minima*, a dwarf species unlikely to exceed 50 cm. in height. This little plant does have a drawback, however. Its flowers are not so elongated and so are less poker-like than are those of the other species. Sometimes, in fact, the flowers of *T. minima* are almost globular. The mace is the symbol of kingship; and the name Reed Mace derives from the fact that Rubens and early Italian painters depicted, in their *Ecce Homo* paintings,

A striking specimen of Rheum palmatum dominates a pond,
with Astilbes in the foreground. This is an excellent example of
a water garden with moisture-loving plants used effectively.

85

the crucified Christ holding the *Typha* reed in one hand. The reed has also a place in Greek mythology. In one legend, the God Apollo, so incensed at King Midas preferring the singing of another to his own, clapped a pair of ass's ears upon the unfortunate king. The king's barber discovered them and felt quite unable to contain so awful a secret. So he hid the secret at the foot of a clump of bulrushes. The reeds could not contain the secret either, and while rustling gently in the breeze, kept murmuring: 'King Midas has ass's ears'. Provided your children are at an age when they can treat fire sensibly, the pokers of the Bulrush can make dramatic torches at a barbecue. Cut the pokers down at the base and allow them to dry indoors. Then soak their heads in paraffin or methylated spirits. Placed in holders around the pond they make a spectacular, if shortlived, form of illumination.

The name bulrush, a corruption of Pool Rush, really refers to *Scirpus lacustris,* a broad and tall plant, too invasive for consideration in a garden. And much as one might admire the dark green, triangular foliage of *Scirpus maritimus* of universal distribution, it is much too vigorous for any setting other than the largest. To be sure, it is a fine plant for attracting wild fowl to your pond. It provides them with excellent cover. But let it be emphasized, water lilies and choice aquatics are not compatible with ducks, which will eat all before them. For the ornamental pond, the obvious choice from the *Scirpus* genus is *Scirpus Tabernaemontani zebrinus.* The plant is known variously as the Porcupine Quill Rush on account of its smooth, slender and sharply pointed leaves, and as the Zebra Rush on account of its very distinctive cream and white bands which ring each leaf from top to bottom. This feature is unique in the plant kingdom. Plant in clumps in shallow water and this rush will grow to about 1.4 metres and will be a most conspicuous element in any pond, especially when the surface of the

The Sweet Flag, Acorus calamus variegatus, showing its peculiar flower spike. The variegated form, incidentally, has slightly less aroma than the unvariegated one.

water is quite still and the bands are doubled by reflection. Should any plain green leaves appear, these should be cut out in case the plant intends to revert to its unvariegated state. Propagation is easily achieved by division. For a striped, rather than a banded effect, include a clump of Manna Grass or *Glyceria aquatica variegata (Glyceria spectabilis)*. It possesses narrow, grass-like foliage striped with no less than three colours: green, yellow and white; in fact four colours, because in spring and autumn a rosy tint creeps into the foliage. In a small basket this lovely plant may grow no more than 30 cm. high. When given all the space it requires, Manna Grass will reach a height of about 90 cm. It spreads rapidly in shallow water and moist soil, so it is as well to restrict its roots.

There are one or two species from the *Juncus* genus which are worth including in the pond. The majority are, as a rule, far too vigorous and tenacious to introduce with safety. The first exception is *Juncus effusus spiralis* which, unlike its relations, is a comparatively modest grower. It is a curiosity plant and the delight of any child. Its leaves grow in wiry spirals, often with the uniformity of a corkscrew. Old timers nicknamed it 'Harry Lauder's walking-stick', for it does rather resemble the crooked walking-stick of that famous Scottish comedian. The second exception is *Juncus ensifolius* which grows 30-50 cm. high. The foliage is rather undistinguished, but towards the end of the summer the plant produces little brown florets which at a distance appear as jet black. They might be the brooms of some miniature chimney sweep. Shallow water or moist soil suits both plants.

If you have a flower arranger in the house, a planting of Sweet Galingale, *Cyperus longus,* will be appreciated, for it is a favourite source of greenery for the florist's art. Its dark green, slender stems which rise perfectly straight for most of their length and then gracefully curve over, make excellent background

The Porcupine Quill Rush, Scirpus tabernaemontani zebrinus, showing some stems reverting to their plain state.

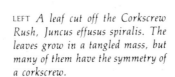

LEFT *A leaf cut off the Corkscrew Rush, Juncus effusus spiralis. The leaves grow in a tangled mass, but many of them have the symmetry of a corkscrew.*

BELOW *Florets of Juncus ensifolius.*

material. And you need never fear cutting off too many of the stems. Sweet Galingale is a trenchant plant and will throw up large numbers of these decorative stems year in year out. The bulbous root, incidentally, is edible. Another highly decorative plant in this genus is *Cyperus alternifolius* or Umbrella Grass. As a native of Madagascar it is not fully hardy, so it should be grown in a basket and wintered indoors. Apart from that, the plant is not fussy, being equally content either in shallow water or on the bank. It grows to about 90 cm.

If you have a summer-house with a wooden or stone floor, then by growing the Sweet Flag, *Acorus calamus*, you can revive an ancient custom. Crush the leaves and they will impart a pleasant perfume not unlike a tangerine orange. This feature of the plant made it highly sought after for strewing over the floor in medieval and Renaissance times. As the leaves were crushed by being walked upon, so the great halls and rooms of olden times were filled with the Flag's sweet aroma. At least so we may believe was the case on occasion, but not always. When the great scholar Erasmus visited Oxford around the end of the fifteenth century, he was not enamoured to find that the rushes on the floors harboured 'expectorations, vomitings, the leakage of dogs and men, ale-droppings, scraps of fish'. But so fond was Cardinal Wolsey of the Sweet Flag that he had the strewings at his palace, Hampton Court, renewed daily. Such extravagance brought the cardinal much criticism. Moist soil or shallow water suit the Sweet Flag equally well and in either situation it grows to about 70 cm. A Japanese variety, *Acorus gramineus,* grows to about half the height of *calamus.* Variegated forms of both are available, the young leaves being vividly striped in green and creamy yellow, fading somewhat to a paler colour in late summer.

When Sweet Flag was in short supply or unobtainable, the odourless Yellow Flag was used instead. Although only second best as a floor strewing, the Yellow Flag has had a rather more elevated history than the Sweet Flag, since Louis VII of France took its lovely flower for use as an armorial device. For this reason it is known as 'Fleur de Louis' as well as 'Fleur de Luce' and 'Fleur de Lis'. Around Orleans in France arose a curious legend whereby it was believed that the seventh son in a family with no daughters intervening, known as a marcon, had somewhere on his body the imprint of the Fleur de Louis and possessed magical powers. Whoever was suffering from 'king's evil' or scrofula had only to touch this imprint or even be breathed upon by the marcon and his malady would disappear.

The Latin name for Yellow Flag is *Iris pseudacorus,* a name presumably chosen to signify its similarity to *Acorus calamus.* The two plants are often found together in the same boggy situations and along river banks, but they are not so similar in appearance. *Acorus* has dark green leaves, comparatively thin and strap-like, often with undulations appearing along the edges for a short distance. The leaves of *Iris pseudacorus* are light green with a distinctive blueish tinge and they are shaped like many sword blades standing with their tips upwards. Although the flowers of this

The Umbrella Grass – Cyperus alternifolius

Although the individual blooms do not last long, the flowering season of irises around your pond can be increased by planting several kinds. The Yellow Flag, or I. pseudacorus LOWER LEFT is a British native and tends to flower in spring; I. sibirica alba BOTTOM FAR LEFT appears in late spring, early summer, and will be followed by I. laevigata 'Rose Queen' TOP RIGHT and I. kaempferi TOP LEFT.

RIGHT The canna lily: one of the most spectacular of moisture-loving plants. However, it really requires tropical or sub-tropical conditions to do well.

iris, like that of almost all irises, evoke a supreme sense of fineness and delicacy, the plant itself is very robust. Possessing a tough and vigorous rhizome, *Iris pseudacorus* is to be found in large numbers in many rivers and wetlands throughout Europe and beyond. If you include it in your pond an energetic programme of cutting back will be necessary from time to time. A more modest grower is found in *Iris pseudacorus variegatus* with its cream and green stripes running the length of the leaf. It has the same flower as the unvariegated form, while a lighter, lemon yellow flower is produced by *Iris pseudacorous bastardi*. Seeds from the ordinary plant very occasionally produce *bastardi*. The plant has the advantage of being unusual if not rare, but the flowers are much less conspicuous than those of the common form. From North America comes *Iris versicolor,* or Blue Flag, which is almost identical to *Iris pseudacorous* except the flowers are purplish-blue instead of yellow. All these irises will do well in wet soil or shallow water and they grow up to a metre in height.

The smaller blue *Iris sibircia* with its grass-like foliage is a particularly versatile plant. It will grow in an herbaceous border with a reasonably high moisture content as well as in a basket submerged in the pond provided its crown is no more than barely covered with water. There are several cultivars of this iris ranging from the deep purple of 'Caesar' to the pure white of 'Snow Queen'. For deeper water, up to 10 cm. above the crown, grow the true water-loving *Iris laevigata,* or *Iris kaempferi.* These two plants need to be distinguished, because whereas *laevigata* relishes water over its crown throughout the year, *kaempferi* does not. *Kaempferi* comes from the rice fields of Japan which are flooded during the summer months and are no more than moist during the winter ones. By growing *kaempferi* in a basket, it can be placed in the pool in spring once growth has begun and remov-

ed in autumn. Otherwise try to find a spot which is boggy but not totally saturated. There are a number of ways in which *Iris kaempferi* and *laevigata* can be differentiated. The leaves of *kaempferi* have a distinctive raised mid-rib which can be easily felt and which *laevigata* lacks (the name *laevigata* comes from the Latin for smooth). The standards of *kaempferi* never exceed two thirds the length of the falls and are often shorter than that. The falls are very broad — the plant's most conspicuous feature — and they often stretch out almost horizontally. The seeds of *kaempferi* are flat, circular or nearly circular discs, contained in a capsule no more than 2.5 cm. long. In *Iris laevigata* the standards and falls are roughly of equal length. The seeds are semi-circular and contained in capsules 5 cm. long. Both these plants require a rich, loamy soil. *Kaempferi* does not like soil that contains chalk or lime while in winter it will appreciate an occasional dose of liquid manure. Propagation is easily achieved by seed or division. Seeds planted in autumn should germinate the following spring, but it may be several years before flowers are produced. It is a good idea to remove the seed capsules in autumn whether or not you intend using the seeds, as this will encourage flowering in the following year.

The tall Louisiana irises, though they can be tempted to flower in the warmer spots of Britain, are best kept for the sub-tropics which is their natural habitat. Hybrids abound and the choice of colours embraces well nigh the entire spectrum. *Iris fulva* is not as conspicuous as some, but is strikingly copper-coloured. Few plants from the sub-tropics can match the Canna lilies for the brilliance of colour — pure red or yellow, or combinations of both. Canna are not strictly aquatic plants as they will grow in ordinary beds, but they do appreciate a high moisture content in the soil and they can be planted in shallow water. They are tall plants, often reaching 1.2

metres, so they need to be planted behind most irises if you are growing clumps of both in close proximity.

Few plants characterise the sub-tropical or tropical water garden more than the Taro plant, with its hanging cordate leaves which have noticeable venation. This species is sometimes called Elephant Ear, not inappropriately. Both the Green Taro, *Colcasia esculenta* and the red form *C. esculenta* var. *fontanesii* grow to about a metre in height, standing in water or moist soil. Papyrus is available in a dwarf form, *Cyperus haspans*, and grows no more than about 45 cm. high. It forms dense clumps of round stems with feathery foliage above.

All these marginal plants can be grown in the pond. Many of them can, as pointed out, be grown in moist soil around it. But there are many more moisture-loving plants which will not tolerate saturated soil. To grow these plants one must think in terms of a bog garden.

The flowers of single and double kaempferi irises, showing the characteristic broad falls and short standards.

93

6 VIRTUES AND VICES OF A BOG GARDEN

Menyanthes trifoliata or bog bean, a low, spreading plant that favours acid conditions.

A bog garden is most often envisaged as simply an extension of the pond. That, after all, is the way it is with nature. Around most lakes and natural ponds lies a boggy area where moisture-loving plants abound. But a gardener, especially the species known as the weekend gardener, should perhaps take a different view. If high on your list of priorities is that your water garden should involve little maintenance and care, then you would be well advised to install a pond only. A bog garden is of course labour intensive. Moist soil is a haven for weeds. There are a number of bog plants that can hold their own against grass and weeds blown in on the wind, *Eriophorum* and *Hemerocallis,* for example; but even a 'wild' bog garden will need more tending than the pool. And besides, a bog garden of this sort will only look right in a large informal setting where there are trees and shrubs to act as a natural backdrop.

There are other considerations too. Bog plants will, obviously, only survive as long as the soil is kept sufficiently moist. If you live in an area of hot, dry summers, maintaining moisture in the soil may be a constant problem, especially if water rationing is involved. A pond and its inhabitants, animal and vegetable, can endure even if the water level drops drastically. Marginals planted in baskets will survive as long as the bottom of the baskets remain in water. (A pond which actually dries up is too shallow in the first place.) But the same weather conditions which would simply lower a well-designed pond, might well dry up the bog garden. And where space is limited I would not be inclined to forego a conventional rockery in favour of a bog garden. A rockery which contains heathers and dwarf conifers — whatever else it may contain — can provide colour and leaf in winter when the bog garden and pond have little to offer.

That is the negative way of looking at a bog garden. In its favour it can be said that a pond and bog garden combined offer a far more varied scheme of gardening, the range of plants is greatly extended; and for anyone who is prepared to involve himself in the additional maintenance, the results can be very brilliant indeed. There is also the advantage that a good number of bog plants are tolerant of shade. This is worth bearing in mind if you have a shady corner close to the pond. If you live in an area of high summer rainfall, the soil round the pond may remain quite moist or damp through most of the year, and the occasional flooding of the pond should therefore satisfy the moisture requirements of most bog plants. Otherwise there are two ways of making a bog garden.

One way is to dig out the site for the pond large enough to include a bog area as well.

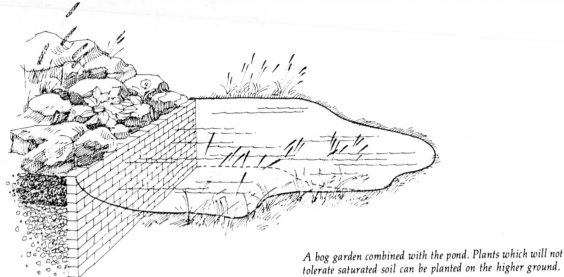

A bog garden combined with the pond. Plants which will not tolerate saturated soil can be planted on the higher ground.

Across one end of the pond is built a dividing wall. This is best done in a concrete pond, but it is not out of the question to build a wall on liners such as Butyl rubber and PVC. One needs to use mortar rather than concrete, i.e. cement and sand but no coarse, sharp aggregate. (The base will need to be broad because the wall will have little or no purchase at either end.) Placing an extra strip of liner under the wall is a sensible precaution. This dividing wall should not be waterproof, but all it needs are just a few small holes to allow water to seep through from the pond without soil passing the other way. The area for the bog garden should be filled with sand (for liner ponds), cinders, gravel, etc., to about 30 cm. from the top of the wall. Above this should be built a mixture of loam, well-rotted cow manure, leafmould or peat, and sand. The loam should make up about half the mixture, and the others should each make up about one sixth of the total. For bog plants which will not tolerate their roots standing in water, build up the bog garden in a form of a rockery at least 30 cm. above the water table. A great advantage of this particular form of bog garden is that it does not have to be watered separately from the pond. Just top up the pond and automatically the moisture content of the bog garden is maintained. But there are disadvantages. Firstly, the rate of evaporation from the pond will be greatly accelerated. The surface of the soil will pass water to the surrounding air and draw up more moisture from the pond at a surprising rate. And that is not to mention the needs of the bog plants themselves. For this reason, this kind of bog garden is only possible if you have a comparatively deep pond, say approaching a metre in depth, although a greater depth would be no disadvantage. Secondly, it is important that the actual surface area of the bog garden should be small in proportion to the surface area of the pond, otherwise you will almost be able to watch the water level drop before your eyes in hot weather. Make the bog garden ten or fifteen per cent of the total pool area, no more. This kind of bog garden is obviously best suited to large pools both as regards depth and surface area.

If your pool is a small one, then you would be better advised to use a different type of bog garden, and in a way it is a simpler one. Dig out a trough about 30 cm. deep and line it with polythene or cement, and in either case the lining should *not* be waterproof. Better still, make the trough 45 cm. deep, the lower 15 cm. or so consisting of a 'V' shaped channel running the length of the trough. Holes in the concrete or perforations in the polythene should be made above the level of the 'V'. The idea is that the liner will hold water up to the level of the 'V', but above that it can seep away to prevent the plants becoming saturated and the soil becoming sour.

95

Virtues and vices of a bog garden

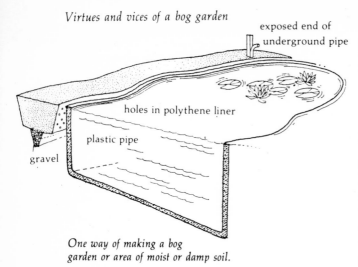

exposed end of
underground pipe

holes in polythene liner

plastic pipe

gravel

*One way of making a bog
garden or area of moist or damp soil.*

This method of making a bog garden offers considerable design possibilities. Do not think simply of digging out a hole adjacent to the pond. If you have it in mind to grow a large number of Primulas, for example, then the bog garden might be designed so as to wend its way round a series of boulders or trees. A circular bog garden with a clump of plants of whatever kind in the vicinity of an informal pond is certain to look artificial. Aim to make the bog garden conform to some specific focal point in the garden or some strong line. If boulders are out of the question and you already have bulbs round your trees, then the best answer might be to make the bog garden conform to the strong curves of the pond itself.

Watering this kind of bog garden can be carried out by overhead sprinkler or hose pipe, but some gardeners employ a rather ingenious method. In the 'V' channel lay down a length of plastic pipe which contains a series of holes at about 60 cm. intervals. One end of the pipe is sealed off and buried. The other end is left open and above ground. All one has to do now is connect a hose pipe to this underground pipe and the entire bog garden can be watered at the same time. Incidentally, the holes in the underground pipe nearest the inlet should not, if possible, be larger than the holes nearest the stopped end. Otherwise the water pressure may not be evenly distributed. And if you bury the pipe in gravel with the holes facing downwards, the chances of the holes becoming clogged will be minimized.

While a bog garden is usually associated with

soil at least 30 cm. deep

rubble

*Formal bog beds made by dividing a pond at both
ends. The fact that the soil would be permanently
waterlogged would limit the range of plants that
could be grown.*

retaining wall with small holes at intervals

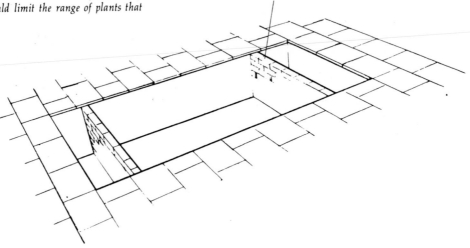

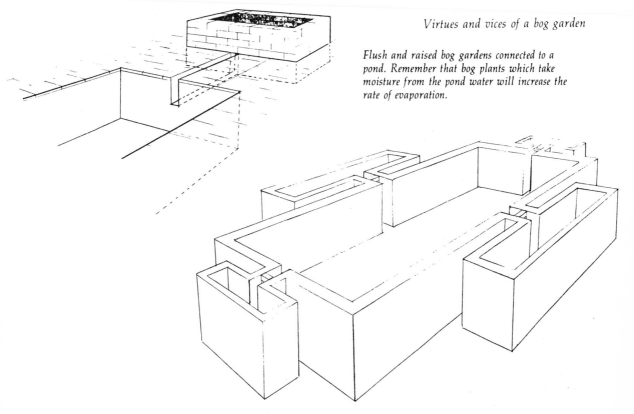

Flush and raised bog gardens connected to a pond. Remember that bog plants which take moisture from the pond water will increase the rate of evaporation.

an informal pond, there is no reason why a formal scheme should not have a formal bog garden , or preferably, to give a more balanced result, several bog gardens. Take, for example, a rectangular pond. About half a metre in from each end could be placed retaining walls to provide two narrow moist beds. Irises look particularly well in a formal design. In the case of a patio pool, bog beds can be sunk in the patio, the bed shape designed to complement the pond. They can be fed by pipe from the pond although this raises the problem of leaking joints. It would be better to join the bog beds to the pond by means of a continuous channel. If the beds are on the same level as the pond then the water level will be the same in both, and this limits one to plants which will tolerate their roots being saturated. Where the pond is a sunken one, then the beds can be placed in the higher ground surrounding the pond. They can still be fed from the pond, of course, but their water table will be lower. Alternatively, the beds can be built up with bricks or cement. The area of the beds below the water table must, of course, be quite waterproof. And to prevent moisture seeping out through the bricks above that level, it is as well to line the whole bed with a liner material.

In the case of a bog garden built like a rockery, the soil on the lowest levels will contain the most water. Begin with plantings of Marsh Marigold, of Bog Arum and Forget-Me-Nots and marginals we have already considered. In addition, plantings of *Mimulus* or Monkey Flowers will provide masses of colour at the pool's edge from summer until the first frosts of autumn. And they will flower even when, through lack of room or soil, they do not attain their full height. *Mimulus* is a primary choice for the small pond. The plant sets seed easily, especially if raised in a cold frame, so that quantities of their showy flowers, rather like open-throated snapdragons,

LEFT TO RIGHT *Mimulus guttatus blotched with red, and hose-in-hose variety.*

can be had in a few seasons. And if that is not praise enough, one can add that *Mimulus* comes in a variety of colours and shapes. Most of the species come from North America, including *Mimulus luteus* which has naturalized itself in Europe. The flowers are yellow. *M. guttatus* is similar except it has reddish blotches or spots on the flowers. Crosses between the two are common. They grow to about 45 cm. but are often a great deal shorter than that. The Monkey Musk, *M. moschatus,* grown for generations for its distinctive perfume, is a creeping plant of low habit. The flowers are pale yellow and not very conspicuous. The plant is mainly suited to very small ponds and has, incidentally, lost its scent. The 'hose-in-hose' varieties are well worth growing, but are not quite as spectacular as *M. cardinalis* whose flowers are a vivid combination of scarlet and yellow. If you want a *Mimulus* that will grow with a few centimetres of water over its crown, then choose *M. ringens,* a species which grows anything from 20 to 90 cm. high and produces flowers of violet or blue. To these, in moist soil, one might add White Bachelor's Buttons *Ranunculus aconitifolius flore pleno,* whose dark green, finely divided leaves will combine beautifully with other plants. And there is a yellow

version, *R. acris flore pleno,* 60 cm. high, which produces lovely double buttercup flowers in profusion throughout the summer.

But for many people the desire to grow bog *Primula* will be the main reason for building a bog garden. *Primula* favour moist, rich but not sodden soil and they certainly dislike sourness. In shade or full sunshine, they can provide a pond with a lightness and gaiety that I do not think is rivalled by any other moisture-loving plant; and they have an ex-

Flowers of the White Bachelor's Buttons, or Ranunculus aconitifolius flore pleno.

ceptionally long flowering period. They are most effective when grown in large clumps, one colour giving way to another. Propagation may be carried out either by seed or division. Immediately the seedlings have ripened, place them in shallow trays containing two parts of loam, two of leafmould and one of sand. Barely cover them with compost and place the trays in a cold-frame, shielded from strong sunlight if necessary. Germination takes place in about four weeks. The seedlings should be pricked out as soon as they are large enough to be separated easily and placed in outdoor boxes, and from there into the bog garden. Many primulas will seed themselves naturally too, and where cross-fertilization takes place you will find new blends of colour and sometimes spotted or blotched forms.

To begin the season early, plant the small Himalayan *Primula denticulata* which will produce globular clusters of lilac, red or white flowers from March onwards. It is satisfied with a modicum of moisture, so it can be placed in the drier parts of the bog garden. For wet soil, the obvious choice is from the candelabra varieties. *P. japonica,* 45 cm. high, produces up to six tiers of the most vivid red to purple flowers in many shades and there is a white form too. *P. beesiana*, a Chinese bog primula, has the distinction of purplish-red flowers with yellow centres. Both these plants seed themselves very readily. So too does the large *P. pulverulenta,* 90 cm. tall with its many tiers of purple flowers. And there are many hybrids available, including the famous 'Bartley strain' of apricot, buff and many hues of pink (right). With the larger pond still in mind, one might add the giant Himalayan Cowslip, *P. florindae,* which also reaches about 90 cm. in height; or what is regarded as a more elegant if less showy form, *P. sikkimensis,* 60 cm. high. The miniaturist might choose the red to lilac *P. frondosa* or the carmine *P. rosea.* Neither of these grows much above 15 cm. But whatever

Primula pulverulenta

For the water's edge, probably the finest fern you can grow is the Royal Fern, *Osmunda regalis*. It does have a regal height, however, and can reach a metre and a half in rich, peaty and moist soil. Better suited to the medium sized pool is *Matteuccia struthiopteris*, or Ostrich Feather Fern, which rarely grows more than 90 cm. high. Its fronds grow upwards in a circular form, looking as much like a giant shuttlecock as the plumage of an ostrich. Its roots are stoloniferous, as are those of *Onoclea sensibilis*, a more vigorous plant though smaller, at 60 cm. on average (in America it is found rather too rampant). It is a fern which will do well in *comparatively* dry situations as

ABOVE *The Royal Fern, Osmunda regalis, situated in partial shade at the water's edge.* RIGHT *An overhead view of Matteuccia struthiopteris, the shuttlecock fern.*

varieties or cultivars you select from this large field — and is there such a thing as an ugly primula? — grow them in scores, all of them. Occasionally one sees primulas displayed in something approaching neat rows in botanic gardens. That is a useful scheme where identification is the first requirement. But the effect is rather stark. In a bog garden, primulas are shown to best effect when combined with other plants. Where space permits, the primula makes an excellent partner with hardy ferns, whose cool, peaceful ambience will heighten the primula's brilliance.

well as in wet, provided it is not exposed to too much sunlight. For finely cut fronds of vivid green, one can hardly do better than choose the well-named Lady Fern, *Athyrium filix-femina*. It grows about a metre high in moist, shaded or partially shaded positions. Rather smaller is the Hardy Maidenhair Fern, *Adiantum pedatum*, generally thought of as one of the most beautiful of ferns. It grows 60 cm. high, requires shade and shelter, and like most ferns appreciates soil rich in humus. This is a useful plant for floral decoration. Equally elegant is *Adiantum capillus veneris*, known as the True Maidenhair Fern, which will do best in deep shade. *Thelypteris phegopteris (Phegopteris*

Sensitive Fern
– *Onoclea sensibilis*

Hardy Maidenhair Fern
– *Adiantum pedatum*

Lady Fern – *Athyrium
filix-femina Cristatum*

Blechnum tabulare

polypodiodes) is well worth growing for its autumnal foliage, which resembles that of the beech tree, hence its common name of Beech Fern. And for foliage which slowly changes character through the year, the young fronds beginning with a pinkish tinge turning to dark green and then to brown, grow *Blechnum tabulare.* It is well suited to moist or wet conditions.

For the rockery, an easy fern to grow is *Dryopteris dilatata* known under the lengthy title of Broad Prickly-toothed Buckler Fern. It is a fern which suits the larger bog garden since it can reach a metre and a half in height. For compactness and a very satisfying shade of rich green, I would include plantings of the Soft Shield Fern, *Polystichum setiferum,* and it only grows about 70 cm. high; moreover there are a number of fine cultivars from which to choose. Of much the same height is the evergreen fern *Blechnum spicant,* whose fronds are divided into narrow pinnae or leaflets which gives the plant a rather wiry appearance. It is a distinctive feature although not one to create the sort of soothing ambience one associates with ferns. To provide a carpet effect, always useful when combining other low-growing bog plants, you might use *Blechnum penna-marina.* The fronds are of a very dark green and only about 15 cm. long. It has an informal habit, some of the fronds growing upright or partially so, others quite prostrate. The plant is evergreen. And so is the strap-

Polystichum setiferum plumosum

like Hart's Tongue, *Phyllitis scolopendrium*, a fern very common in parts of the British Isles and Ireland. There are many variations of the common form, *cristatum* for example in which the ends of each frond are conspicuously divided; and if you have a rustic bridge, a rocky waterfall, little nooks or crannies in the rockery, then this is the fern with which to fill them. Another is *Polypodium diversifolium*, a native of Australia and New Zealand, with long, finger-like fronds. Many ponds are built in the vicinity of dry stone walls. If you want a dainty fern for such a position, then *Asplenium trichomanes*, the Maidenhair Spleenwort, will meet your need.

Ferns loomed large in folk lore. Once it was believed that the little folk went trysting, borne aloft on aerial steeds made of fronds. Another belief was that whoever could capture the seed of a fern, which made its appearance only at midnight on midsummer's day, would receive magical powers. Ferns also played

LEFT *The Hart's Tongue Fern takes many forms. The buckled appearance of the fronds on this plant is its most distinctive feature.* BELOW LEFT *Blechnum penna-marina, a fern of low habit which makes it useful for rockeries and for combining with other small plants.*

Polypodium diversifolium

a part in love potions (they can be poisonous, in fact). The old beliefs are gone, but to walk through a glade of ferns is to know that their mystical atmosphere remains.

Hosta is another plant that combines well with *Primula*. It likes a rich, deep, moist or damp soil but is not particular as to sun or shade. The plant is grown primarily for its broad and compact leaves, the flowers in many cases being uninteresting and sometimes partly hidden between the leaves. An exception is to be had in *H. ventricosa*, whose large purple to blue flowers rise well above the leaves. But its overall height of 90 cm. makes it rather too large and bulky for many gardens. *H. lancifolia*, 60 cm. high, with dark green though not particularly broad leaves, is more suited to the smaller bog garden. Preference might be given, though, to *H. glauca*, which has glaucous leaves of rich blue, or *H. glauca fortunei* (also called simply *H. fortunei)*

whose leaves are less blue but whose pale lilac blooms appear on top of tall stalks. For dramatic effect, you might choose *H. fortunei marginata alba*, whose dark green leaves are edged with white or cream. This is a most conspicuous plant. Do remember, however, that if you are growing the variegated forms of such plants as *Acorus calamus, Iris pseudacorus, Scirpus* and so on, the effect of green and cream and white, endlessly repeated, can be rather overpowering. One can have too much of a good thing.

The new pond owner almost always overlooks grass-like plants in favour of more colourful ones. This is a pity. They provide the water garden with a dignity few other plants can equal. This is especially true on calm, still days when the reflection of muted colours in the pond will evoke a sense of placidity which irises, for example, by their very colourfulness cannot do. Moreover, plants whose beauty lies in their leaf and shape are

of two metres and more — are the largest that can be grown in temperate zones. The plant itself can reach a height of 4.5 metres. A native of Brazil, *Gunnera* is named after J. Ernst Gunner, a versatile individual who combined the roles of bishop and botanist. Doubtless it is the very massiveness of the plant which has made it so popular, although it is not fully hardy. To protect from frost it needs to have its leaves doubled over the crown in the autumn and this will provide it not only with protection but with a mulch. No other treatment is necessary. However, to my mind, unless planted in a spacious garden and unless its site is congenial and the plant attains its

LEFT *The mighty Gunnera manicata well situated on a large expanse of water. Its extraordinary flower spike* BELOW *can be a metre or more in length, and 30 cm. in diameter.*

attractive throughout the whole growing season. If you are not including Sweet Galingale *(Cyperus longus)* in your scheme, then *Carex stricta* or *pendula* will create the same elegant effect. So too will the lovely *C. riparia* 'Bowles' Golden' which needs very wet soil or shallow water and grows no more than 40 cm. high. More than most plants, these sedges will give the impression that your pond has existed for years: they mature the scene. And for the larger scheme, Pampas Grass, *Cortaderia argentea,* has a warming as well as a maturing effect. The plumes are white or silvery and sometimes touched with lavender, while the plumes of the less well known *Cortaderia quila* have a definite lavender hue and are, if anything, even more feathery. They are excellent subjects for reflection close to the pond. Coming from South America they appreciate a certain amount of shelter.

Perhaps no other plant is more often grown where it is ill-suited than the mighty *Gunnera manicata*. Its leaves — which can attain a width

LEFT *Hosta lancifolia*

true proportions, *Gunnera manicata* looks like nothing so much as a rhubarb plant that has got beyond itself. Beside a small or even medium-sized pond, *Gunnera* appears not so much a dominant, imposing plant as a clumsy intruder. It is only in the context of a vast expanse of water that the true magnificence of this plant becomes apparent.

And much the same can be said about the rhubarbs, such as *Rheum palmatum,* whose deeply lobed leaves create a fine impression of opulence on a plant that can reach 2.5 metres and more, and which produces panicles of creamy white flowers. *Rheum palmatum atrosanguineum* has leaves even more deeply dissected and magnificent flowers of brilliant crimson. But the owner of the small garden would be best advised to resist such glories and include a dwarf species such as *Rheum inopinatum,* 60 cm.

high. Not that the compromise is a great one; this little plant has conspicuous red veins and stems with greyish-green leaves and scarlet flowers. *Rheum,* conveniently, likes to be left undisturbed for years and does best in rich, moist soil and some shade. More shade and less moisture suits *Rodgersia,* a genus much admired for both its foliage and flowers. *Rodgersia pinnata alba* has dark brownish-green leaves and white flowers, while *R. pinnata elegans* has a more bronze tint in the foliage and red flowers. As neither of these plants is likely to exceed 60 cm., they can be accommodated in most schemes.

And no bog garden of whatever size should be without a few varieties of *Astilbe.* Few moisture-loving plants are more obliging as regards situation and none is more spectacular. Any soil will satisfy these plants and while

ABOVE *Goat's Beard, Aruncus diocus, makes a striking display by the waterside where space permits.* RIGHT *Astilbe x Arendsii.*

106

An informal pond with dense planting of marginal plants around the sides. The marginals are growing in a 'trough' formed by a random stone wall set on a ledge in the pond. The space between the wall and the bank of the pond is filled with soil. The result is very natural but maintenance is high as weeds thrive in the saturated soil, species of juncus especially, and also grasses. (Author's own garden)

107

they respond to plenty of moisture in summer, very satisfactory results can be obtained in less than optimum conditions. Their flowers are borne in soft, feathery and pointed plumes. The flowers of the large *Aruncus sylvester (Spirea aruncus)* and the smaller fine-leaved *A. kneiffi* are not dissimilar to those of *Astilbe*. And the flowers of *Rodgersia* and of *Spirea*, although lacking the same pointed tops, are often confused with *Astilbe*. All these plants are well worth growing for their soft, fluffy plumes, as is the Double Meadowsweet, once classified as a *Spirea* but now called *Filipendula ulmaria plena*. But what can equal the radiance of *Astilbe* blooms caught in the bright sunshine of a summer's day or their soft, glowing colours contained in a shady glade? Astilbes bloom from June to August and varieties abound. There is a fine choice of colours in the *Arendsii* cultivars: pink, red (p. 106), white and mauve, ranging in height from 60 cm. to 1.8 metres; and there is a little Japanese form, *A. simplicifolia*, which is only 22 cm. high. It produces a little frothy

Rodgersia aesculifolia

spire of pink flowers. Propagate Astilbes by division.

No less easy to grow is *Hemerocallis*, derived from the Greek 'for a day', hence the common name of Day Lily. Despite the short life of the individual bloom, the Day Lily flowers over a long period, and if a number of different hybrids are planted, one can expect blooms to appear all summer long. They need little or no tending, improve with the years, and they are forceful enough to defeat a multitude of weeds. *Hemerocallis* comes in innumerable hybrids mainly of orange and yellow, but also of pure white. Like *Astilbe*, *Hemerocallis* thrives in moist soil, but I feel these plants should not be placed together, although this is often recommended. The light green foliage of the Day Lily is justly admired, but it is altogether coarser than the finely divided leaves of *Astilbe*. Moreover, the flowers of the Day Lily are strong and definite rather than light and fluffy. To combine these two plants is, to my mind, rather like laying a table with both pottery and cut-glass. Certainly there is room for *Hemerocallis* and *Astilbe* in the same bog garden, but divide them by rocks or ferns. And if you want a companion for the Day Lily, choose from among the cultivars of the Globe Flower or *Trollius europaeus*, whose yellow, white and orange blooms will mix well, while their globular shape will add an element of contrast.

And whatever selection you finally make among the many bog plants available, apply the same rule to them as to marginals. A series of large plantings of several plants is better by far than smaller groups of many. Resist the temptation to buy too wide a variety of plants. Having stocked the pond with water lilies, marginals and bog plants, one can now turn one's attention to another dimension altogether: that of fish and animal life.

Bog Cotton, Eriophorum angustifolium, is a conspicuous plant which is easily grown in wet or damp acid soil. The white tassels of bog cotton waving in the wind are a splendid sight, but you need lots of them to make a show.

Golden Orfe, Idus idus, one of the most popular of pond fish. They are easy to keep and are fond of cruising along on the surface.

7 FISH AND LIVESTOCK FOR THE POOL

There was a time when many ponds were referred to, especially by monks, as 'carp-pools'. For adjacent to many a monastery lay a pool well stocked with carp. Those fish often grew to a prodigious size, and when a meal was required, a monk or retainer simply netted a basket of fish. Refrigeration and improved transport put an end to the practice. But carp are still to be found in public and private lakes and ponds. The native Asian Carp, *Cyprinus carpio*, was introduced to Europe a long time ago. It averages about 30 to 40 cm. in length, but specimens 100 cm. long and 20 kilos in weight are not unknown. The Asian Carp is easily distinguished from the European Crucian Carp, *Carassius carassius*, by having two barbels on each side of its upper jaw. Carp are extremely tame and will often cruise to the surface well within reach. I sometimes wonder how many of them may have provided a meal for some hungry poacher or tramp. There is no reason why one should not keep these friendly creatures in a largish pond except that their dark colour makes them rather inconspicuous. And they revel in rooting in the bottom of the pond and tearing up aquatic plants. So far as carp are concerned, the obvious choice for the ornamental pond is from the numerous varieties of goldfish *(Carassius auratus)*. There are over one hundred recognized types — all relatives of the humble carp.

Regardless of the varieties you choose, do select healthy fish. There is no difficulty in identifying them. A goldfish in the peak of condition will have an erect dorsal fin and his movement will be definite or vivacious. A sick fish will lie on the bottom, be motionless or almost so; and if he is not capable of swimming upright or keels over at all, then do not buy him. Presumably, you will transport your fish home in a polythene bag with water taken from the tank in the shop. This water may well be at quite a different temperature to the water in your pond. Fish are cold-blooded creatures which means they adapt their blood temperature to that of the surrounding water. They can survive in extremes of temperature, but they cannot adapt instantly from one extreme to another. So, rather than release your fish immediately into the pond, allow the polythene bag, with the neck open, to rest in the pond until the water in the bag is within a few degrees of the water in the pond. Then simply tip the bag over and release the fish. He should then dart off to hide in a clump of weed, under a rock, or if he is a larger specimen, he may begin exploring the pond immediately. And it is best not to introduce fish to a new pond until the underwater plants are growing well. This way one knows that the water is in fit condition for livestock.

The utter stillness of aquatic plants, especially the water lily, in a way begs the constant motion of fish. If you have had the opportunity to become used to both in one pond, then you will almost certainly feel something is missing in a pond which has only one of these elements. And the relationship is not solely an aesthetic one. Fish may be chosen primarily for their ornamental value but they are also useful scavengers, protecting lilies from the onslaught of insects, among other creatures. They are worth including in a pond for this reason alone. And no fish is more beautiful nor more effective a scavenger than the Golden Orfe *(Idus idus)*, which is also available in a silver form. Long, slim fish that quickly grow up to 30 cm. and more, they tend to move in shoals especially when small and can whip and dart through the water at great speed. More important, they spend much of their time at the surface, will readily take floating food including insects, and are on view frequently. Their characteristic flight through the water makes for a very satisfying contrast to the more languid, peaceful movements of the common goldfish which are, however, even more tame. Indeed it is not unusual for goldfish to become so tame that they will feed directly from the hand. Once this practice is established, as soon as you appear the fish will congregate at your feet. So too will Shubunkins or Calicoes which are varieties of goldfish, but which come in multicolours of red, black, brown, purple, white and most highly prized — and priced — of all, blue. They appear almost scaleless on account of the fact that their scales lack pigmentation. Shubunkins are also available in single colours and are very conspicuous fish.

A fine specimen of Shubunkin

Breeding grotesque and outlandish forms of goldfish has been brought to a fine art in Japan and America. Veiltails or Fantails have squat, fat bodies with long flowing tails usually in three sections and often as long as the head and the body put together, indeed sometimes longer. The Black Moor also has great bulbous, telescopic eyes. So highly developed has the finnage of some of these fish become it is almost inoperative. Veiltails and Black Moors can only strut through the water like so many fat duchesses. This can be a problem if the fish is dependent upon food you throw into the water. Golden Orfe and the common goldfish easily outstrip them in speed, so special provision has to be made for them to be certain they do not starve to death. In a well-established pool with plenty of underwater plants all fish should do well enough grubbing for midge larvae, algae and other natural foods. Fantails and Black Moors are more susceptible to ailments than ordinary goldfish. In particular the air bladder, situated in the centre of their squat bodies, which controls their sense of balance, often gives rise to problems. If you are attracted by their long, flowing tails, but feel the Fantail is too ungainly or troublesome, then a compromise is possible in the Comet Goldfish. Their conspicuous tail fins are about a third of the length of their bodies, but short enough to be functional. They are very agile fish. All sorts of combinations of fancy characteristics have been bred into goldfish apart from elongated finnage. There is the Bubble Eye, and the Celestial Goldfish whose eyes are situated on top of its head. But to my mind the most grotesque of all are Lionheads and Orandas, which have large warts on their heads like seeds of corn-on-the-cob. The more perfect the symmetry of the finnage of these goldfish, or the more highly developed their grotesqueries, the more expensive they come. In a pond, as opposed to an aquarium, where one is normally looking down at the fish from some distance,

the finer points of symmetry are not apparent and one is as well off buying the cheaper, less perfectly shaped specimens. Symmetry is no indication whatever of the health of a fish, although it can be said that the more squat the body the more vulnerable is the fish to ailments.

Golden Orfe are not likely to breed in the average pond, but goldfish will breed readily during warm spring conditions. It is possible to buy goldfish in breeding pairs at extra cost. But this is hardly necessary as any five or six fish are almost certain to contain both sexes. Come the warm weather and the females or hen fish who are ready for spawning will develop fat, rotund bellies, while the males, or cock fish, who are ready for mating very often develop a pattern of small dots on their gill plates. A temperature of 15°-18°C. is favourable to spawning. The mating ritual consists of males frantically chasing a female round the pond, chivying and nudging her flanks encouraging her to spawn. Often this ritual goes on for hours at a time. Sometimes the female is cornered and almost forced out of the water. Occasionally her flanks can become torn from friction with rocks or the walls of the pond. This can lead to fungal infection, especially if the female is exhausted by so much attention. That, however, is the way with nature. In time the eggs are deposited usually on dense weed in shallow water and the male fertilizes them. Several spawn-

A Water Bubbli, or Bubble Eye, a somewhat delicate fish, better suited to aquarium culture.

ings may occur over a period of ten days. Depending upon the temperature the eggs will hatch in about three to five days. The fry are tiny, no larger than the head of a pin. It may be several months or even the following season before you spot them: thin, translucent initially and only a few millimetres in length. Fish are notorious cannibals and it is an advantage to have a shallow area in your pond in which the young can take refuge — in theory, if not always in practice, the larger fish will stick to the deeper areas. As they mature, some of the fry will take on the colour or mixed shades of their parents; others, unfortunately, will revert to the plain blackish-brown of their ancestors. Some may, in time, lose this dull colour in favour of red or yellow, but for a certain number black or olive brown will be their permanent colour. In commercial breeding, selection procedures are adopted and bright red hues are encouraged by the use of chemicals and high-temperature tanks. So far as pond fish are concerned, one has to rely on natural sunshine. But this does not mean preventing the fish from having adequate shelter in terms of rocks and weeds, which are essential to their well being. In an aquarium, artificial lighting may encourage fish to change colour, always provided, of course, that the individual fish has that potential. Again it is important to ensure that the fish have adequate cover should they want to use it.

Goldfish rarely suffer from underfeeding but are vulnerable to being fed too much too often. In winter, fish in an outdoor pool hibernate, hidden among the weeds, emerging only during warm, sunny spells. They require no feeding at all during this time and any food they look for can easily be found amongst the weeds. In summer, in addition to fish pellets and other patent foods, fish are grateful for an occasional diet of chopped worms, if you can bear to chop them, *Daphnia* and a portion of a hard-boiled egg that has

been very thoroughly chopped up or minced. But whatever you feed your fish, never give them more than they can consume within about fifteen minutes. If food is left lying around, not only will it discolour and possibly pollute the pond (boiled egg is a particular danger), but it is a sure indication that the fish are being overfed. In a well-planted pool, the base of which is almost covered with oxygenators, feeding is hardly necessary at all. So you can limit the expense of buying fish food to those occasions when you want to bring the fish up to the surface and close to view, and to tame them. Feeding in spring may encourage your fish to breed; while in autumn it should build up their strength for winter. Of particular value to fish fry are the minute organisms known as infusoria associated with decaying vegetable matter. Infusoria can be prepared by taking a little water from the pond in a jar and suspending in it a bruised and rotting lettuce leaf. Spinach leaves, lentils, the dead leaves of water plants and even a banana skin will serve the same purpose. Best results are likely to be obtained if the water temperature is around 22°C. or above. After a few days you can judge whether infusorians are present by holding the container up to the light. The water should appear as if filled with a greyish-white dust. These are the infusorians. Simply tip the contents of the container into the pool, preferably at roughly the same temperature as the pool water, to prevent killing the culture.

To have seen the Koi carp (p. 122) is to have seen the most magnificent of all pond fish. Unlike Shubunkins, their scales are very obvious and pronounced and their colours are even more striking, especially the golden form. There is no more brightly coloured ornamental fish available. The golden form is truly the colour of gold, not merely a shade of yellow. And Koi are not simply tame. They are fearless. Dip your fingers in the water and immediately you can expect your hand to be

113

The Oranda goldfish, showing the splendid finnage.

surrounded by Koi, all clamouring and jockeying for position in the expectation of tit-bits. They grow to great sizes, and a pond containing five or ten Koi, each weighing upwards of two kilos, is an unrivalled sight. You could, however, buy a three-piece suit for the price of one such fish, and still have change in your pocket. Better to begin with small fish and feed them up. Koi grow quickly. There has to be some drawback with fish so strikingly beautiful, and it has to be said that while Koi can thrive (at least a small number of them) in a garden pond, they do best and are seen to best advantage in a somewhat specialised environment, which is discussed in the next chapter.

RIGHT *The Catfish is as ferocious as it looks. Although they are often sold by aquarists, on no account introduce them to a pond containing other fish.*

Green and Golden Tench (*Tinca tinca*) will live in harmony with goldfish and are often recommended for ponds on account of the fact that they are scavenger fish, eating detritus and grubbing around in the bottom of the pool. The fact that they can survive in water with a low oxygen content makes them easy to keep. But being bottom feeders they are rarely seen in a pond which has an adequate planting of weeds; and their value in mopping up dead snails and keeping the pond clean is probably over-estimated. Similarly, the little Bitterling *(Rhodeus amarus)*, 8 or 9 cm. long, and the Gudgeon *(Gobio gobio)* are not likely to be seen or noticed. On the other hand a small shoal of Minnow *(Phoxinus phoxinus)* is an attractive feature. True, their colour is nondescript, but their activities, flitting around, suddenly seen in one space only to disappear into a clump of weeds and reappear somewhere else, make them worth keeping. Apparently their habit of scattering — as opposed to staying together — in the face of danger, is a tactic for survival. It is believed that a predator is unable to concentrate his attention on one particular minnow when a shoal scatters in all directions.

And the Stickleback *(Gasterosteus aculeatus)* is certainly worth including, not only for its subtle colouring of red and blue lines along the flank, but also for its characteristic movement and above all for its unusual life-style. The stickleback always appears as a very self-possessed little fish, thrusting itself through the water at great speed and then pulling up sharply to remain motionless until it gets it into its head to take off again, and again pulling up dead as if attached to some miniature and invisible braking system. At mating time, usually from early spring until midsummer, the female loses her greeny black colour for a shade of yellow; and the male's flank takes on a strong red hue, his back a bright green and his eyes become electric blue. He then sets about collecting small pieces of vegetation which he glues together in some nook, and this serves as a nest. The glue is secreted from the kidneys. An elaborate courtship follows during which the female or females are enticed into his parlour to lay their eggs.

RIGHT *The Great Pond Snail, Limnaea stagnalis. Note the egg rope laid by another snail being carried on its back.*

Once the nest is full of eggs, the female stickleback has no further duties. The male takes charge of the eggs, fertilizes them of course, aerates the water in their vicinity by vibrating his fins, and protects them and the hatched fry until they are old enough to fend for themselves. Any young stickleback who tries to leave the nest before father approves is taken in father's mouth and thrust back into the nest. Sticklebacks are not, contrary to what is sometimes said, a danger to other species of fish. They keep their aggression for defending their territory against other sticklebacks. The same is certainly not the case with the ferocious catfish, which will eat all before it. For the same reason, under no circumstances should the Brown Trout (*Salmo trutta*), the Common Perch (*Perca fluviatilis*) or the Pike (*Esox lucius*) be introduced into ponds which contain goldfish.

About introducing such predatory fish with goldfish there is no debate at all. Trout, perch and pike will devour the goldfish. About introducing snails and mussels, opinion is somewhat divided. If your interest in a pond embraces the creatures it can support as much as the plants, then snails in their various shapes and colours, their behaviour and egg capsules, will undoubtedly add to that interest. Snails are valuable in that they eat decaying vegetable matter and perhaps serve a purpose in keeping the pond free of pollution. Not all of them, however, limit themselves to decaying matter. The Great Pond Snail, *Limnaea stagnalis*, is very partial to Frogbit, oxygenating plants and the leaves of water lilies, especially the smaller plants. This snail can be easily recognized by its conical shell 5-6 cm. high. Keeping it out of the pond entirely is almost impossible. *Limnaea* are hermaphrodite or bisexual. This means that not only can a 'male' and 'female' reverse their roles at will — they often do during courtship, especially if two snails are joined by a third — but a single snail

The Three-spined Stickleback, Gasterosteus aculeatus

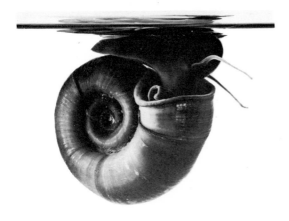

Great Ramshorn Snail, Planorbis corneus, on the water surface, showing its tentacles and siphon.

can fertilize its own eggs. The implication is obvious. If one *Limnaea* gets into your pond, it can quickly raise a colony, laying egg capsules as long as itself and containing up to 300 eggs. *Limnaea* very often succeed in entering new ponds, either the snail or its eggs being carried in surreptitiously on aquatics or marginals. But there is no need to attempt to eradicate them, even if that were possible; keeping down their numbers will solve any problems. The Ramshorn Snails are often recommended for ornamental ponds because they do not eat lily leaves and the like. They have shells which are not conical like *Limnaea*, but are flat. It is worth introducing the Great Ramshorn, *Planorbis corneus*, a red-blooded snail about 35 mm. wide, or its more decorative relation, *Planorbis corneus rubra* which has reddish rather than a black or brownish shell. Under suitable conditions these snails can breed at a prolific rate while under others they may not succeed in breeding at all. One can only try introducing a few and seeing if your pond has the right conditions.

Mussels too are particular about their environment. They require the presence of mud. Where plants are rooted directly in the soil in the base of the pond the mussel offers a hazard. When it moves round it tends to uproot oxygenators in its path. (Their movement can be curtailed by building up a circular wall of stones which they will be unable to cross.) In their favour it can be said that a mussel continually siphons water while feeding off the algae. In this way a few mussels can be a great help in keeping a pond clear. The contention that a dead mussel offers a serious threat of pollution is probably exaggerated, unless one is talking about a sink pond or the like. But if you want to introduce mussels into your pond, you would be well advised to introduce one species only. That is the Zebra Mussel, *Dreissena polymorpha*, which is about 2 to 4 cm. long and is banded in two shades of brown. The larvae of this mussel do not attach themselves as parasites on passing fish as some mussels do; and the mature Zebra Mussel is not liable to uproot plants.

No risk is attached to the introduction of frogs. And no creature, to my way of thinking, adds a greater sense of homeliness to the garden pool. Their appearance in the pool every spring to breed, the pleasant, often frenetic activities of the tadpoles, the occasional hopping and prancing of the young frogs when disturbed in the undergrowth, all add to the sense of the pond as a centre of life. But not everyone will agree. About the Common Frog *(Rana temporaria)*, the Edible Frog *(Rana esculenta)* or the Marsh Frog *(Rana ridibunda)* most people have a very decided opinion. They are found either delightful or repulsive. Their shiny skins in muted colours, their squat bodies and sad liquid eyes are not found equally appealing by everyone. If you find nothing especially attractive about these creatures, tolerate one of the species for its usefulness in eating pests.

In Britain, the frog population has been drastically reduced due to the drainage of areas of marshy ground during agricultural and urban reclamation. School biology lessons have made children everywhere familiar with frogs. In North America the common species is the Leopard Frog *(Rana pipiens)*.

The Common Toad — Bufo bufo. For some reason Koi carp do not care for the tadpoles of toads.

This versatile frog can stand extremes of temperature and is found as far north as Canada and as far south as Mexico. As the name would imply, all Leopard Frogs are heavily blotched or spotted, but their overall colouring varies from grey through green to brown. The Leopard Frog grows to about 12 cm. in length and like the massive American Bullfrog *(Rana catesbeiana)*, 20 cm. long with legs up to 25 cm., it is renowned for its prodigious jumping ability. A good specimen of Leopard or Bullfrog in energetic mood can leap a distance of 1.4 m. and more. The Bullfrog has the unusual characteristic of guarding its tadpoles which will cluster round the parent for safety. Such cautious behaviour is probably necessary as the tadpoles may remain as tadpoles for up to three years, and that is a vulnerable stage in a frog's life. Adult Bullfrogs will spend their lives in or close to still water, unlike the Wood Frog *(Rana sylvatica)* which favours damp woodland areas, except when visiting ponds in spring to breed. It grows to little more than 8 cm. in length and is widely distributed through the south-eastern states of America to as far north as Alaska. The colouring of the Wood Frog is very variable, ranging from brown, black and yellow to a pinkish colour. Obviously, the Wood Frog is suited primarily to ponds with a natural woodland setting, and the Bullfrog is rather too large for the small garden pond.

Where space and food supply may be limited, a more congenial species and one common to ponds and streams in the north-eastern states is the Green Frog *(Rana clamitans melanota)* which may grow to no more than 8-10 cm. Despite its name it can be brown as well as green and is blotched. An even smaller version, the so-called Bronze Frog *(R. clamitans clamitans),* is found further south.

The American Toad *(Bufo americanus)* deserves respect for its voracious appetite for mosquitoes; while the Common Toad *(Bufo bufo)* and the Natterjack *(Bufo calamita)*, both native to Europe, have a useful diet consisting

The Common Newt – Triturus vulgaris

of caterpillars, beetles and other pests. So does the Common or Smooth Newt, *Triturus vulgaris* 6-8 cm. long and widely distributed; and the Palmate Newt, *Triturus helveticus*, which is widespread in Western Europe but less easy to find. The hind feet of the male Palmate are webbed and his tail ends in a thin filament. The Great Crested Newt, *Triturus cristatus,* is the largest European species, growing 12-16 cm. long. It has a rather warty appearance. Secretive, agile creatures, newts come to the pond to breed in spring or summer, as do toads. The Great Crested Newt is the only newt which may remain in the pool to hibernate during the winter. The others leave after breeding and may roam far and wide. They are most likely to be seen in hot weather when they leave their secret haunts in water to sunbathe. There can hardly be a child who is not enthralled by their appearance, especially in spring when the males are at their most colourful. All newts shed their skins from time to time, rather in the manner of snakes but with greater ease. Sometimes an entire transparent coat is to be seen floating in the water, that is, if the newt has not devoured it. Newts can sometimes be caught by drawing a worm on the end of a piece of string through the water of a wild pond. Often a newt will hold on to the worm and it can then be brought to the bank. Newts make excellent aquarium pets where their mating ritual can be observed and the females' habit of folding the leaves of submerged water plants over each individual egg can be watched. They are best returned to the outdoor pond or to the wild in mid-summer. In America, the Japanese newt, *Cynops pyrrhogaster,* has become a popular pet.

If you intend keeping Veiltails and Black Moors an aquarium is almost essential. These delicate fish (like many other hybrids) require comparatively high temperatures and should be over-wintered in an indoor aquarium. You could also bring in the young fry of the goldfish as a means of separating them from their predatory elders. And there is the added advantage that with an aquarium there is no closed season. Instead of your fish hibernating, hidden in the depth of the pool, you can enjoy their graceful lives and those of many other creatures in your own house during the winter, and at close quarters.

A typical plastic moulded aquarium

8
KOI CARP AND FILTRATION

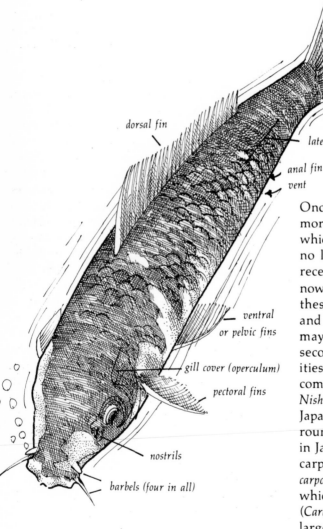

dorsal fin

lateral line

anal fin
vent

ventral
or pelvic fins

gill cover (operculum)

pectoral fins

nostrils

barbels (four in all)

Once was the time when a water garden was more or less a synonym for a lily pond to which a few goldfish were usually added. But no longer, for the popularity of Koi carp in recent years has meant that many ponds are now specially designed for the exhibition of these splendid and magnificent looking fish; and water lilies and aquatic plants, such as may exist in a Koi pond, are very much a secondary consideration. In effect the priorities as between plants and fish have been completely reversed, though Koi carp, or *Nishikigoi* as they are also called (*nishiki* being a Japanese word for coloured cloth), have been round for a long time, having been first bred in Japan early in the nineteenth century. Koi carp derive from the Common carp (*Cyprinus carpos*), as opposed to the common goldfish which is a descendent of the Crucian carp (*Carassius carassius*). Koi grow a great deal larger than goldfish; Koi of 90 cm. and more have been raised and fish of 60 cm. are common, whereas goldfish do not usually exceed 40 cm. and are generally much smaller (not that size is necessarily the only or most important consideration as regards beauty and enjoyment of keeping fish). The life expectancy of Koi under the right conditions is probably around fifty or sixty years, although claims for very much longer-lived fish have been made. Domestic or cultivated goldfish might live for thirty years or thereabouts. A mature Koi is not easily mistaken for a goldfish, not only on account of its normally brilliant coloration but because the head and 'shoulders' are much stouter; but certain identification of Koi lies in the fact that they have two pairs of barbels protruding from above the upper lip, whereas goldfish have no barbels. Both the Common carp and Crucian form are generally black or brown in colour, but mutations sometimes occur; and it was from such mutations that the present varieties of goldfish and the ever expanding range of coloured Koi have been developed.

In Japan in particular the breeding of Koi has been pursued as both an art and a science, the activity of life-long study, the stuff of PhDs. and closely-guarded secret techniques. Koi in Japan have pedigrees stretching back generations in the way that race horses and dogs have elsewhere. At the top end of the market a prize Koi could be worth the price of a family house! At the other end of the market small Koi, without impressive pedigrees or rare colour combinations or markings, are within reach of anyone and can be kept in the garden pond; though if the pond has been especially designed for keeping Koi it is only to be expected that they will fare better.

The remarkable rise in the popularity of Koi has brought in its wake the now widespread practice of installing filtration systems, some quite complex, in domestic ponds. The point is worth making, however, that it is not absolutely essential to have a filtration system in order to keep at least a few Koi. They will survive under normal conditions; but the problem with Koi is their propensity to snuffle in the mulm and detritus at the bottom of the pond, clouding the water, and their habit of eating soft vegetation such as floating and underwater plants, and occasionally uprooting water lilies and the like. If you wish to maintain a large number of Koi in water that is transparent, so that you can see their wonderful colours to best advantage, then the pond should be designed for that purpose and filtration will be an essential part of it. A filtration system can, of course, be used in a pond with or without Koi. To some people underwater plants are unsightly, and their function of purifying water can be carried out by a concealed filter, and the water oxygenated at the same time. It has to be said, however, that a pond without underwater vegetation will have nothing like the diversity of creatures that you usually find in a 'natural' pond, even if man-made. Water boatmen, pond skaters and many more such creatures (admittedly some that attack fish fry) are likely to be absent or few in number; and I, for one, find a pond without such creatures, however pure the water, a little on the sterile side. Koi, incidentally, make short shrift of the tadpoles of frogs — toads seem to survive better — so if you want to sustain a tadpole population you may find it necessary to partition your pond, shifting the frogspawn to the area free of Koi. There is no reason why a filtration system should not be combined with a pond conventionally stocked with underwater plants, and by this means you can have the best of both worlds, the diversity of pond life with less underwater plants than would otherwise be necessary. There is more free space in which to view your fish and you have sparkling clean water at the same time. It is largely a question of designing a pond and filtration system according to what you want. A pond specifically for Koi is a specialised environment, and the Koi fancier is not likely to be concerned with making his pond a habitation suitable for anything else.

ABOVE *This is the kind of view you can expect of your Koi during feeding time. In the picture below can be seen a Taisho Sanke and, lower, a Shusui. Although Koi of two or more colours are much in demand, there is much to be said for single-colour forms as well. The Golden Ogon* RIGHT *is a particularly brilliant variety.*

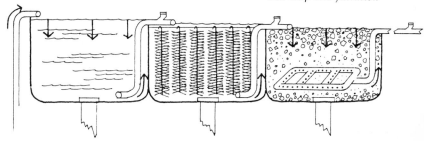

Typical multi-stage tank consisting of settling tank, tank with brushes, and a gravel tank. Other combinations are, of course, possible.

Filtration

Filtration can be by mechanical, chemical or biological means. It is common practice to combine at least two of these methods in any one system. Mechanical filtration is the means of removing solids from the pond water: mud, dust, organic matter, etc.; for anything which is larger than microscopic in size there is a chance of removal by mechanical means, for example, by use of a settling tank. Water is pumped slowly from the pond into a tank, where solids sink to the bottom of the tank as the water slowly passes back into the pond or is transferred to another filter (see drawing). It is important that the water, as it enters the settling tank, is not turbulent and swirling round, otherwise the solids will remain in suspension. Remember that the narrower the bore of the pipe you use, the greater the velocity of the water. It is to reduce the velocity that pipes with comparatively large diameters, 76 mm., 100 mm. and even up to 250 mm. on occasion, are used for filtration purposes — the very opposite to fountains, where the 'squirting' effect of water is achieved by narrow bore pipes creating jets of high velocity. A settling tank which is 10 per cent of the volume of your pond would probably be ideal but may not be practical, for if you intend using other filters as well (multi-stage filters as they are sometimes called) you could end up by assigning a very large portion of your garden just to a filter system. Never mind — a settling tank can still be effective even if much smaller than the ideal; it will depend largely upon the amount of solids you are trying to clear. But

for the sake of argument a pond with a volume of 10 cubic metres might have a settling tank as large as .75 to 1 cubic metre. You then have to decide how fast the water should pass through the settling tank, which can be expressed as the turnover rate of the water in the pond. Obviously the slower the water moves the greater will be the amount of solids that will settle out. On the other hand, if you are using a multi-stage filter a comparatively fast turnover of water is desirable, even as fast as a complete turnover of the pond water every hour. This is likely to be too fast for your settling tank, so a compromise is necessary, say a turnover of two or three hours. Assuming a turnover rate of two hours, then you can calculate the required output of your pump as follows: 10 cubic metres (the capacity of the pond) is the amount that will pass through the settlement tank in two hours. The turnover in one hour, would be $10 \div 2$, which is 5 cubic metres, or 5000 litres per hour (approx 1100 Imp. gallons); and that is the required output of your pump.

The advantage of a settling tank to remove solids is its comparative cheapness, especially if it forms part of a multi-stage filtration tank; but it is by no means the most efficient method of removing solids. With a sand filter the turnover of water can be faster, but the system is much more expensive. Water is pumped into the filter via a multiport valve, and returns to the pond through further multiport valves laid in coarse silica sand, with further layers of finer sand above. The tank is

123

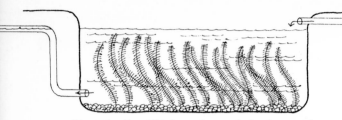

Vegetation filter. The denser the growth of underwater plants, the more efficient the filter in terms of mechanical and biological filtration. A filter of this kind, unless very large, is useful primarily for its mechanical effect.

specially designed to withstand pressure so that the water can be forced through the sand. A means of backflushing the tank is incorporated in these systems, and the back-flush outlet should be connected with a drain. Sand pressure filters are commonly used for swimming pools but are useful for Koi pools too. Sand as a filter medium is fairly easy to keep clean, whereas diatomaceous earth, which is sometimes used, is not. The size of your sand pressure filter and pump should be matched to the volume of your pond, so follow the guidelines of the manufacturer.

A cheaper alternative to a sand pressure filter is one that uses a material such as finely spun glass-fibre wadding, polyester or a similar mesh. A tank or cylinder of the material is connected in line with a pump — the tank can be submerged in the pond — and will collect solids quite efficiently. When the wadding becomes heavily soiled it is taken out, washed, rinsed and put back in the cylinder. This kind of filter is often used to protect pumps, in addition to the mesh guard that usually covers the inlet to the pump, and a fibre filter can be useful where small ponds are concerned in helping to keep the water clear. Polyester fibre filters have, of course, been used for many years in aquaria, and what are aquaria but miniature indoor ponds? In fact nothing more than a small fibre filter, with or without charcoal (which helps to purify water), and an aerating stone, can provide a healthy environment in an indoor tank. Obviously if the water in your pond is very clouded you will have to clean the filter

more frequently than if the water is reasonably clear. There is no reason, of course, why two or more filters of this kind should not be employed.

There is one other method of filtering out solids that is well worth considering. Instead of a settling tank, you could have one heavily planted with a densely growing underwater plant such as *Elodea canadensis (Anacharis)*. Such a tank would operate in exactly the same way as a settling tank, except that instead of the solids sinking to the base, they would adhere to the *Elodea* which is extremely effective as a filter (see drawing). Every now and again the flow of water can be stopped, the *Elodea* brushed with the hand to disturb the adhering mud, and the cloudy water drained off. The pump is then started up again. Spray the plants with a jet of water to remove the mud if you prefer. Almost any underwater plant will have some filtering effect, but those with the bushiest growth will be the most effective, *Elodea*, *Egeria* and *Myriophyllum* being among the best. While the effect of this method of filtering is primarily mechanical, the underwater plants simply acting as an obstruction, the plants would, nevertheless, have some effect as regards purifying the water; and of course the Koi cannot get at them.

Mulm and detritus that collects on the floor of the pond will not be filtered out, except in so far as the Koi snuffle and churn up the mud on the bottom, which is exactly what you want to avoid. So Koi keepers often install one

In a large pond two or more bottom drains can help to minimise the build-up of mulm and detritus on the pond floor. Make sure the bottom slopes towards the drains.

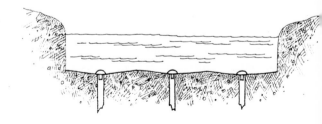

or more bottom drains in the pond, each drain being set in the centre of a concave area so that the mulm settles round the drain. Some Koi keepers make a point of changing a proportion of the pond water on a weekly, even daily basis, say 10 per cent per day or 25 per cent per week; 10 per cent per week in winter. But the trouble with changing pond water at all is that many water supplies now contain chemicals which are highly toxic to fish. Chlorine will evaporate in a day or two, and if you can manage to have a standing tank then your pond can be filled from that; but this of course adds more to the cost of your set-up and there is always the space factor to be considered as well. Chloramine, which is now found in water supplies in the United States, can be lethal to fish. It can be neutralised by such products as *DeChlor*, which will render chlorine harmless too.

Chemical filters such as zeolite act by neutralising the toxic effect of nitrites and ammonia which build up from fish waste. Water is passed through the granules of zeolite, pumped from the pond and, after percolation, returns to the pond by gravity feed. Zeolite will not function indefinitely without cleaning, and it is necessary from time to time to remove the granules, place them in a salt solution for several hours and then rinse them thoroughly before returning them to the tank. To avoid disrupting the filter, a second, clean batch of the granules can be kept ready. There is a problem with zeolite, however. If the granules are allowed to become dirty, they then cease to function as a purifying agent and in fact have the opposite effect, encouraging the build up of toxins in the water. So this kind of filter is one that requires careful watching and regular maintenance.

But all these methods of filtration are secondary to what Koi keepers regard as the most important means of filtering and purifying water: the method known as biological filtration. It consists of building up bacteria on a suitable medium in suitable quantities, so that the bacteria can purify the water that passes over them, converting the metabolic waste product of fish (primarily ammonia, which is extremely toxic to fish) into less harmful constituents including nitrites and nitrates. It is a complex process in which the conversion of ammonia and other waste is carried out by bacteria of different kinds, one producing nitrites, another turning the nitrite into nitrate. What the pond keeper needs to remember is that these bacteria require a continuous supply of oxygen, which is to say that they are *aerobic*, and a steady flow of water is essential to sustain the bacteria. If you lift a stone out of a stream you will notice that it has a slippy feel to it. This is because the stone is covered with aerobic bacteria, which create the ecological balance found in clear water streams. This is the effect you are trying to create in your own pond. Should the flow of water over the bacteria medium stop for any reason, such as pump failure, the oxygen level around the medium will very rapidly decline, the bacteria may die off and in their place *anaerobic* bacteria may form. The result would be conditions toxic to your fish. So in the event of your filter tank remaining full of still water for any length of time, other than a few hours at most, you should take the tank out of commission and thoroughly clean the filter medium before connecting the tank up to the pond again. Because oxygen-rich water is so important to these nitrifying bacteria, as they are called, it is usual to incorporate in the filter system a means of increasing the oxygen content in the water. When you first set up your biological filter, it will take a number of weeks, even months, depending upon many factors including water temperature, before the bacteria spread, cover all the available surface area of your filter medium and do their work. However, the medium can be 'seeded' with freeze-dried

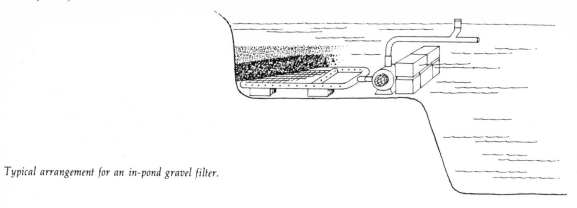

Typical arrangement for an in-pond gravel filter.

bacteria which are commercially available, and this speeds up the process. You should then have an ecosystem, self-sustaining, which should operate for some years without any disturbance other than the draining off of solids or backflushing of the tank, depending upon the system you have adopted.

Any inert material is suitable as a culture medium for bacteria, but obviously the more surface area the medium has, the greater the number of bacteria that can be supported and the more efficient will be your filter. For instance, a rock of a given volume would have much less surface area than a load of gravel of the same volume. Gravel, not surprisingly, is a popular filter medium, particularly if you want to incorporate the filter in the pond itself. Gravel made up of 6 mm. particles is what is generally used, and should remain undisturbed by the fish; if needs be, you can cover over the gravel with a fine mesh. The usual arrangement is for an area of the pond to be walled off with submerged bricks to contain the gravel (see drawing above); or, alternatively, you can design your pond so that it has a suitably deep depression in the centre. It is very important that the flow of water through the gravel is spread evenly, rather than in 'tracks'; so a network of perforated pipes are laid out in the gravel medium, preferably with a plastic mesh covering, and this pipework is then connected

up to your submersible pump via an under-gravel adaptor. The idea is that the pump draws the pond water downwards through the gravel, and the outlet of the pump can be directed anywhere round the pond. If you have water lilies you should try to minimise the currents in their area, as *Nymphaea* like still water. If the outlet pipe is above water the ripples created on the surface will help to aerate the water. But if this appears un-aesthetic you can keep the pipe completely

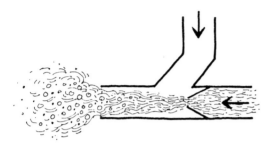

The principle of the Venturi.

Filter media by Cyprio Ltd.

submerged and still aerate the pond water very effectively by means of a device known as a venturi, named after its inventor, the Italian physicist, Giovanni Battista Venturi (1746-1822). This device is simplicity itself — you can easily make one yourself — and depends upon tapering pipework to create a vacuum, at which point air is drawn into the pipe and mingles with the rushing water. It only requires some PVC piping and couplings, and a blowlamp to heat and taper the end of

ABOVE *A typical filtration tank. The lateral bar across the top of the tank is the spray bar; a larger tank would require a number of such bars. This tank is used with optional open cell foam, OPC, with plastic filter media beneath.* LEFT *An in-pond filter tank, showing two layers of open cell foam with gravel media beneath.*

one pipe, to make a venturi, or you can buy one and tap it into your system.

The advantage of an in-pond gravel filter is the ease and cheapness with which it can be made, and there is not much plumbing involved. It does have the serious drawback, however, that if something does go wrong with it, you have to disturb the pond in order to tackle the problem. A gravel filter can be made in a tank beside the pond, and it will operate in exactly the same way except that the submersible pump remains in the pond and pumps water up to the filter, and the water is gravity-fed back to the pond. Alternatively, if you do not want to have your filter tank exposed above ground level, the process can be reversed, the water being fed from the pond to the tank by atmospheric pressure and pumped back to the pond. In the absence of a separate overflow pipe (installed as a precaution), it is important that the rim of the filter tank is at least as high as the top of the pond, otherwise if the pump should fail, the filter tank will overflow.

Gravel is an extremely cheap medium with which to make a biological filter, and used in the pond it has the advantage of not being too easily disturbed by fish. But if you intend having an external filter then you may well think it worthwhile to invest in some of the other filter mediums which have advantages that gravel does not. Baked clay granules, also

127

known as horticultural aggregate, are light and easy to handle. So too is processed rock lava which, having many pitted surfaces, offers a greater surface area for the growth of bacteria. Synthetic sponge with its innumerable minute holes has become a popular medium for small pools, and is often sold with tanks already plumbed and ready for use. If you are buying sponge separately make sure it has not been treated with a fire retardant which can be toxic to fish. Sponge will also act as a mechanical filter, and if your tank is fitted out with several layers of sponge, then the top layer can be removed from time to time for rinsing without the main body of the filter being disturbed.

Another medium which has a certain mechanical filtering effect as well as providing many surfaces for bacteria to grow on, is long-bristled brushes, a Japanese development. These brushes are suspended in quantity in the tank. A certain amount of mud and detritus will adhere to the bristles — just as would be the case with brush-like underwater plants were you to set up a 'vegetable filter'— and all you have to do is shake the brushes occasionally while the flow of water through

Typical filter brushes as suspended in the filtration tank. The more bristles, the greater the number of bacteria the brush can support.

the tank is temporarily stopped, and then drain off the mud held in suspension.

Yet another filter medium which has become popular, on account of being both cheap and very convenient to use, is nylon mesh, identical to pot scrubbers except for the fact that each filter is tied securely in its centre to prevent unravelling. These filters (made by, among others, Spong & Co. of Essex. England) can be simply dropped into the filter tank; they will not clog up as gravel, horticultural aggregate or sponge has a tendency to do, so there is no need to have a means of backflushing the medium, and the solids will collect at the bottom of the tank.

A point always to remember is that biological filters require a great deal of oxygen; indeed, this point can hardly be overstressed, and water leaving the filter tank is likely to be deficient in oxygen. If you are not using a venturi connected into the inlet pipe then use spray bars. Have another venturi connected in the outlet pipe; or use what is known as a mat aerator, basically a cylinder containing turbine vanes which mix air and water together. A waterfall or fountain, powered separately, or yoked up to the filter — the filter water can be returned to the pond via a waterfall — is all to the good, the splashing, the ripples and general turbulence all helping to aerate water.

All the materials and elements required for filtration can be bought as complete sytems; or you can build your own single or multi-chamber tank to your own specifications and lay out the plumbing exactly as you want it, and make a significant saving in the process.

Once you have your filter going, let it operate for a little time to allow bacteria to build up before introducing your Koi. The textbook way is to build up your stock of Koi slowly. A quarantine tank in which to keep newly acquired fish for some weeks is a precautionary way of avoiding infection in the main pond.

Size of filter

It is important that your filter is large enough to do the job required of it, and that the flow rate through the filter is adequate. Ideally the volume of a filter tank should be as much as 10 to 15 per cent of the volume of the pond, and the entire volume of water in the pond should pass through the filter tank once every hour. If that sounds complicated, it is not so difficult to work out in practice. To take an example: let us say your pond measures 4 metres long by 3 metres wide by 0.9 metres deep, then the volume of your pond is 4 × 3 × 0.9 = 10.8 cubic metres. If you want a filter tank which is 15 per cent of the volume of your pond, make the calculation:

$$\frac{15}{100} \times 10.8 = 1.62 \text{ cubic metres.}$$

We know that the volume of the pond is 10.8 cubic metres and that the water should be recycled every hour, so the output of the pump should be 10.8 cubic metres per hour or 10,800 litres. The equivalent in US gallons would be the litre figure divided by 3.7854, which in round figures is 2800 US gallons per hour. If you buy a pump with a flow rate slightly higher than that (to allow for head loss if the filter tank is raised above the pond, and friction loss in the pipework) it is an easy matter to reduce the flow rate by means of the valve. There are sophisticated ways of measuring flow rate, but for our purposes it is quite satisfactory to let the filter tank flow into a bucket of known volume. 10,800 litres per hour is what is required, which works out at 3 litres per second (divide by 3600). It would be better to use a slightly longer period of measurement than one second, if the bucket or receptacle is large enough, say 15 litres in 5 seconds (3×5). Adjust the valve on the pump until you get the figure you want.

The dimensions and flow rate given here are what one might aim at to achieve optimum results. In many instances so large a filter tank (combined perhaps with further chambers) is just impractical and a pump in continuous operation is an expensive charge on one's electricity bills, not to mention the capital cost involved in setting up the filtration tanks. Good results can be achieved with smaller tanks and a slower rate of recycling the water, especially if you do not 'overload the system' by overstocking your pond.

Koi: rules to follow

The question as to how many Koi a given size of pond can accommodate is a vexed one, really more pertinent to the commercial breeder than to the home owner of Koi. Different figures are given, experts differ in their opinion, but under good conditions you could have a stocking rate as high as 15 cm. of fish per 0.09 sq. metres of pond surface. But to my mind the beauty of Koi, or any other fish, is compromised if the setting in which they appear does not seem spacious. That does not necessarily mean having a large pond, but it does mean keeping down the number of fish to reasonable numbers. You do not need a mathematical formula to determine this: the eye is the best judge. Besides, overcrowding in a pond is a likely cause of ill health among fish.

The British winter is not notably harsher than the Japanese one, but winter in Britain lasts appreciably longer and this can undermine the health of Koi. The problem in parts of the United States and Canada is compounded by both duration and severity. One answer is to bring your fish indoors, though this is not a practical solution if you have a collection of sizeable Koi. The use of a pond heater works well enough when the frost and ice is of short duration; over long periods it encourages fish to frequent the warmed-up area, which increases their metabolic rate. At the same time they will be exposed to much lower temperatures elsewhere in the pond, and the sudden changes may undermine their health. A better practice is to cover a section of your pond with polythene supported by boards raised above the surface of the pond. A novel and effective idea is to incorporate a building of some sort over your pond, though this of course requires a pond of some size.

Koi can tolerate quite a range of temperatures, but in common with goldfish and many other species do not like rapid changes in temperature. For this reason a pond deeper than is necessary for growing *Nymphaea* is to be recommended, although in mild climates Koi may well thrive in comparatively shallow ponds. The Koi specialist, however, will have an area, if not his entire pond, at least 0.9 metres deep and very likely 1.2 metres deep or more.

Koi have voracious appetites and feeding twice daily is a good practice. If you cannot manage to be regularly available, it is possible to buy automatic feeders. However, Koi should not be overfed; floating pellets should not remain uneaten on the surface — a sure way to add to the pollution problem of a pond. Feed your Koi from the same vantage point each time and they will soon learn to associate that area of the pond with being fed, and will readily take food right from your hand in a short while. Floating pellets is the ideal way to encourage Koi to come to the surface, and pelleted food is made to a large range of recipes. So-called staple pellets provide a balanced diet of fish meal, protein, minerals and so on; wheatgerm pellets are said to be readily digestible even in low water temperatures when the fish are less active; pellets containing carotene and *spirulina alga* are fed to Koi to improve their colour density. Mini pellets are available specially for small fish, and a sinking pellet has been designed for when the fish are reluctant to come to the surface, either on account of the weather or from fear of your presence. However, if the weather is that cold, Koi should be fed very little indeed; and Koi will not long remain shy of you, especially once the association is made between your presence and food.

Koi carp are classified according to colour and markings, and a descriptive list of some of the varieties can be found in Appendix IV.

This picturesque chalet (which contains a heated swimming pool) overhangs the pond by perhaps two metres, so providing the fish with shelter during harsh weather. The bridge would also provide protection. The designer has struck a nice balance between the size of the chalet and the pond.

The common heron, a beautiful sight on a river or estuary, a dreaded sight by a pond.

9 PITFALLS, PROBLEMS AND POND CARE

Cracks and leaks

If you were to ask ten water gardeners what they considered to be the worst problem associated with ponds, you would probably receive but one single answer from all ten. A pond that leaks constitutes the worst problem.

No water, obviously, means no pond. Fortunately, leaks are rarely so severe as to leave a pond empty. But any leakage that is discernible creates problems. The constant topping up of the water level with the garden hose is not only an added chore, but also adds unnecessarily to the chemical content of the water upon which algae thrive. Tap water will also tend to chill the water in the pond which in turn will reduce the vigour of the water lilies and they may not bloom so freely. Evaporation during the hot days of summer is bound to lower the water level to some extent, and topping up cannot be avoided entirely. Leakage may increase the amount of topping up to an unsatisfactory degree. And finally, a leaking pond often means the inconvenience of having an area of lawn or pathway which is constantly soggy.

It cannot be overstressed that if a pond is to be made of concrete, it must be made to the highest standards. Improperly mixed materials, the inclusion of foreign, organic matter such as leaves in the mix, insufficient reinforcement, can all lead to a leaking pond, be it on account of porosity or of cracking. Firm foundations are essential too. Little wonder therefore that flexible membranes, which can be overlaid with a protective layer of concrete if desired, have all but superseded the concrete pond as far as the home gardener is concerned. However, concrete can now be repaired without undue difficulty using a proprietary sealant or a rapid hardening cement. If the crack is a large one, grout it first with stiff mortar; or if the concrete has broken into unstable 'platelets', remove them and grout the gaps with fresh concrete before proceeding with the sealant or rapid hardening cement, which should be spread over the joints and for a fair area on either side of them.

Sometimes a new home owner is confronted with a garden full of enormous boulders — the garden may be essentially an outcrop of rock — and there is no possibility of removing them. To simply concrete round such boulders where a depression exists is likely to lead to leaks between boulder and concrete. Again the use of a sealant or rapid hardening cement should make it possible to 'marry' rock with concrete.

Liner ponds will not crack, but they are probably more vulnerable to children who enjoy 'messing about with water'. And what child does not enjoy playing beside, and given the chance, in water? A broken glass, a garden fork, not to mention the innumerable knick knacks with which children play, are all a potential means of puncturing the skin of Butyl rubber or PVC. To be sure, these materials can take a certain amount of prodding and misuse, nevertheless the possibility of a puncture is always present. Puncturing may also occur if any sharp stones or the like are not removed from the foundation before the liner is placed in position. Land movement also offers a hazard: sharp stones may become exposed which had been concealed before. A subsidence of soil in the base or even the sides may leave a hollow beneath the liner and should someone step into the hollow then the liner may be forced to stretch beyond its elastic capability and a tear is inevitable. And the walls of the liner should not be placed under too much tension. Make certain the liner is lying smoothly over the *entire* base and fitting snugly into the corners. When making a raised pond this point should be particularly noted, as the temptation is to raise up the liner a little so that the sides are taut. Repairs to Butyl rubber and PVC are permanent, but do not underestimate the trouble involved in finding and repairing a leak. It requires emptying, cleaning and drying out the pond, and it may involve examining the liner centimetre by centimetre until the leak is located. Perhaps the old saying: 'prevention is better than cure' was concocted by an old pond builder!

Whatever depth you make your pond, obviously it would be fatal to the fish if the water were to freeze in its entirety. The fact that a pond freezes over will not in itself cause problems for fish, it is factors associated with freezing that can undermine and sometimes kill fish. For one, fish cannot respond quickly to rapid changes of temperature, so weather which fluctuates widely between being mild and warm to severe and very cold can prove fatal. Secondly, a pond that is completely frozen over retains its toxic wastes and so ice can be the cause of fish suffocating. The more organic matter you have decomposing in your pond — leaves are the obvious bugbear in this regard — the greater the level of toxic waste there will be. Netting the pond during the annual fall of leaf is a sensible precaution, and saves the remedial work of cleaning out the pond later. A pond heater will keep a small area of water free of ice from which toxic gases can escape. Alternatively, cover a section of your pond with a sheet of polythene raised above the surface with planks. Areas with very severe winters, where a pond might be expected to be frozen over for several months, may not be suitable for such treatment. Overwintering of fish indoors may be the only solution.

Snow lying on ice is another problem that needs to be guarded against in severe climates, as the absence of light penetrating the water can mean oxygenators die off. Brushing the snow off at least a section of the pond should reduce this risk.

Plant ailments

So much for the actual pond; water lilies and marginal plants are susceptible to few ailments. Nymphaeas may sometimes suffer from a fungus disease of the genus *Cercosporae*. This is comparatively rare, but when the fungus is present, spots will develop on the leaves which became dry and crumpled. A light spraying of Bordeaux mixture, applied every other day at half the strength directed for other plants, is the only remedy. The affected leaves should, of course, be removed. But do not mistake the natural decay of leaves for this fungus. If healthy leaves are rising to the surface and developing as others are dying off, then this is only evidence of the natural cycle of events. And, of course, once autumn frosts have arrived you can expect the Nymphaeas to die back quickly.

A peculiarity of some water lilies is the phenomenon known as fasciation. An individual plant may grow and flower normally for a number of years. Then, for no apparent reason, it ceases to bloom and instead of producing leaves of usual size, it throws up a much larger number of tiny leaves. If you lift the plant you will discover, instead of just a few separate and well-defined growing points, a jungle of leaves and shoots growing all over the tuber. Fasciation is rare, but when it occurs there is only one solution. Remove any eyes or shoots that appear normal. These can be planted and should grow into ordinary tubers which will flower and produce leaves of the usual size. The original tuber can be discarded.

Reverting to type is a tendency that you may notice with some of your variegated

marginals. In amongst the variegated foliage plain green stems may develop. Given time, the whole plant may revert to the plain colour of its ancestors and you will have lost the variegated species with which you began. The only thing you can do is cut out the plain stems as they arise and hope that the rest of the plant will remain true to type. The fact that the variegation on the leaves of *Iris pseudacorus variegatus*, for example, may lose some of their lustre, the green and bright creamy stems taking on a duller appearance at the end of summer, is not evidence of reverting to type, but only of the ageing process of the leaves. Should any straight leaves appear on *Juncus effusus spiralis*, they also should be ruthlessly cut out.

Plant pests

Much more of a nuisance than either of those problems are the pests which attack the leaves and tubers of water lilies. Among these can be included: aphids, especially the reddish-black one, the Water lily Aphis, *Rhopalosiphum nymphaeae;* the larva of Caddis flies, *Trichoptera,* and of the Brown China Marks Moth, *Nymphula nymphaeta.* Aphids lay their eggs on the leaves of water lilies and the larvae feed off the leaves. The China Marks Moths lay their eggs near the edge of leaves or underneath them and the larvae are quite capable of destroying the foliage. The larvae of the Caddis fly, in its protective suit of armour, crawls about the bottom of the pond and can sometimes damage the tubers of water lilies and their buds. To say as much about these pests is to conjure up a picture

The Brown China Marks Moth, Nymphula nymphaeta, has white wings with brown markings. The caterpillar of this moth builds for itself a watertight case made of leaf fragments and silk. The case is attached to the underside of leaves floating in the water. During the winter the caterpillar hibernates, but in spring it feeds hungrily off adjacent vegetation.

Caddis larva (Phryganea species) emerging from its case.

The Caddis larva (Limnephilus species) case BELOW is made of shells, tiny stones or grit and pieces of wood. Contrary to what is sometimes claimed, it is not possible to identify species from the materials which make up the protective cases. Certain species do show general preferences in choosing their materials. This case is about 25 mm. long.

of a pond ravaged and denuded. The extent of the problem is very much a matter of luck. These insects may be quite rare in one area and quite common in another. But the remedies are both simple and effective. The most important one is fish; have your pond well-stocked with young, vigorous goldfish and Golden Orfe, and they will feed readily off these insects and their larvae. The leaves of water lilies often rise well clear of the surface and the upper portion of all floating leaves will, of course, be out of the reach of the fish. So you can aid the fish in two ways. Spraying the leaves with a firm jet of water is one way: the insects are forced into the water. The other is to spread a net over the lily leaves and submerge them by holding down the net with weights. Placing plants in a bath of Derris is sometimes recommended. But the cure may prove worse than the pests. Derris is highly toxic to fish and unless all traces of the insecticide are washed off the plants before returning them to the pond, you may find yourself minus your fish stock. I would use such a measure only in the most extreme of cases. Where aphids are a particular problem, cut back the dead foliage of marginals hard and burn it. The adult insects hibernate in the hollow stems of waterside plants. Finally, the Freshwater Snail, *Limnaea stagnalis*, will often develop a taste for leaves and sometimes buds. However, given the choice, this snail prefers the head of a lettuce or a cabbage stump to water lilies. Place one or two of these plants in the water on a few successive nights and simply remove the snails attached to them. Surplus snails are quickly eradicated in this way.

As regards floating plants — the Water Soldier and Frogbit in particular — pond owners are sometimes baffled by the fact that they had a plentiful supply in one season only to find that they have none in the next. What had happened? It is possible that the plants simply rotted away at the end of the summer.

But the owner's own conscientiousness may have been his undoing. The Frogbit spends the winter months as small, insignificant buds resting on or immersed in the mud on the bottom of the pool. Similarly, the Water Soldier may only survive the winter in the form of little bulblets which grew and separated from the mature plant in summer. In cleaning out a pond in autumn one can unwittingly throw out these plants. It is not a bad idea to collect them before they sink to the bottom and transfer them to a jar of water. The same can be done with the seeds of *Trapa natans*, the Water Chestnut (but it will hardly ever set seed in the British Isles or Ireland).

Cleaning the pond

Talking of cleaning a pond, how thorough should one be? Even if you grow all your plants in baskets, it is inevitable that the base of the pond will, in a short time, receive a layer of mud and debris and probably small stones. In the case of liner pools the stones are worth removing for fear of damage. But a certain amount of mud is unavoidable and there is no point in continually removing it. Pond maintenance means preventing pollution above anything else. The decay and putrefaction of water plants and the leaves from nearby trees, especially in a small shallow pond, can destroy the quality of the water and can prove fatal to fish. Any sign of an oily sheen on the surface of the water is evidence of some degree of pollution. Never allow the water to reach the stage you often see in dykes and ditches of becoming a smoky blueish colour. If it does the oxygen content is likely to be very low indeed and a very thorough cleaning-up operation is needed. But your pond should never reach that stage. An occasional clearing of dead leaves during the summer, a thinning of oxygenators from time to time, and a cutting back of dead

foliage in autumn is really all that is required to keep the pond healthy — a self-perpetuating eco-system. Some owners of concrete ponds lower the water level from time to time to scrub the walls clean of algae — liners can be washed and rubbed down too — but I would only carry out this operation very occasionally, if at all. A certain amount of algae is always present. It can best be kept in check by underwater plants; but if blanket weed forms this should be removed by hand or twirled out on the end of a stick.

Fish ailments and pests

Fish are susceptible to quite a few ailments and pests; but one pest constitutes a greater threat than all others combined. And sadly, I know of no satisfactory remedy. That pest is the heron. Should you happen to live anywhere near a river or heronry, then sooner or later your pond is likely to be visited by one of these birds. Even a small sheet of water is very conspicuous from the sky and a heron in the vicinity can hardly fail to notice it. They are shy birds, easily frightened by the appearance of human beings. But what they lack in courage they certainly make up for in perseverance. At odd, quiet hours, especially around dawn, a heron will not hesitate to land in a built-up area if he knows there is food for the taking. Goldfish are easy prey and a heron can devastate, indeed wipe out, one's entire stock of fish. If he does not do so on one visit, be assured he will return so long as there are more fish to be caught. In my experience, the most likely time for this unwelcome visitor to arrive is in winter when food may be scarce, especially after heavy rain when the local river is in a muddied spate.

In many countries, herons are protected by law. And rightly so, for they are graceful, lovely creatures in flight, and their tranquil, placid silhouette on many a river bank or estuary — if not in the garden — is surely a

RIGHT *This picture is not upside down. The Water Boatman, Noto-necta glauca, is suspended from the water surface.*

LEFT *The Great Diving Beetle, Dystiscus marginalis; a greedy, carnivorous creature with a life span of several years. They are about 30–35 mm. long in the adult stage, and the larvae, which are even bigger, are also predatory.*

sight worth preserving. A small pond can be netted over in winter, but again the heron may arrive when the net is off; and if you are growing plants around the margin of the pool, then you have the added irritation of the plants growing through the net in early spring before you may feel it is safe to remove it. And bear in mind too that a heron has no compunction about sticking his long beak through netting with even small holes. I have known the birds both to walk on plastic netting and raise it up at one corner. So the netting should be firmly secured at the water's edge and raised above the pond by placing a pole or similar object in the centre of it. An electric wire, similar to the kind of thing used for cattle, with a low voltage, may deter herons; but how permanently I cannot say. They are wily and persistent birds, and while I know of a pond containing Koi which has been successfully protected in this way, it is not inconceivable that a heron might learn to avoid the wire. Deep water and a high bank above surface level is doubtless a deterrent but hardly practical for the average garden.

LEFT *A Water Scorpion, Nepa cinerea, feeding on a damselfly larva.*

The notion that a model of a heron — even a male in mating dress — deters visitations of the real thing should be regarded with scepticism. Perhaps the only way of keeping out herons other than to keep your pond netted when you are absent, is to net over the whole garden or the water section of it.

Cats take a malicious pleasure in standing by the pool's edge and whipping fish out. Friendly fish who come up to the surface on the sight of a human being may well do the same for a cat. A well-aimed missile will put off most cats from repeating the experiment.

There are a number of insects which may attack small fish and fry. The Great Diving Beetle, *Dystiscus marginalis*, and others of the genus, are carnivorous and will feed off fish, snails, tadpoles and insects. They fly from pond to pond so they cannot be entirely excluded. The Water Boatman, the most common of the species being *Notonecta glauca*, has a powerful pair of stylets with which it can make short work of tadpoles and small fish. The Water Scorpion, *Nepa cinerea*, takes hold of its victim with a strong pair of front legs and then sucks

A dragonfly larva revealing its ferocious face mask.

137

the blood of its captive like a vampire. The larva of the dragonfly possesses a so-called mask, a kind of jaw with powerful hooks. These are used to snatch and grip passing prey, fish being among the victims.

To prey and be preyed upon is part of the unalterable cycle of the pond, indeed it is of the essence of all natural life. To break the cycle is well nigh impossible. Hand picking or removing by net a number of these creatures is possible — in particular the Diving Beetle — but their eradication is not. From the many eggs that mature goldfish may lay and which hatch out, only a tiny proportion reach adulthood. Only the most stringently controlled conditions can raise the survival rate significantly. The pond owner must, I think, be satisfied with the way of nature in what is a relatively natural environment, unless it is a special Koi pool that you have, in which case predators would have to be ruthlessly controlled, especially if you are intent on breeding fish. Adult fish can be expected to contain the population of these enemies. And although enemies to fish, the activity of the Water Boatman and the Water Scorpion as they scurry about the pond, as well as many other insects, is surely an intrinsic element of interest in any water garden.

Remedial action should, however, be taken in the case of an infestation of Anchor worms or fish lice. The Anchor worms attach themselves to the skin of the fish and there is usually a slight swelling at the point of entry. They can grow up to almost 2 cm. Fish lice are very much smaller, 5-6 mm., and when they attach themselves to a fish, it is common to see the fish dashing wildly around the pond for no apparent reason. In both cases remove the affected fish and, holding it firmly in a wet cloth — but without squeezing it unduly — take out the parasite with a pair of tweezers. Treat the point of entry with iodine or a little household disinfectant; or paint the parasite with paraffin oil which will kill it. Examine

the rest of your fish stock and treat in the same way as necessary.

These parasites may be introduced with plants taken from the wild. Before placing in your pond, new plants can be disinfected with potassium permanganate. A few grains of the chemical in a bucket of water in which the plants can be submerged will serve the purpose. A complete pond can also be disinfected, and potassium permanganate will also cut down the algae growth and improve the clarity of the water. The danger is, of course, that the fish will be poisoned by the chemical, fry in particular, and so far as clear water is concerned the measure can only be regarded as temporary. So I would use it only as a last resort. Make up a saturated solution of the chemical and introduce it to the pond at the rate of two teaspoonfuls for every ten litres of water.

White Spot is the common name of another parasite made evident by the rash of white dots that may run over the skins and fins of the fish. It should not be confused with the little dots that may appear on the gill plates of cock fish during the mating season. It is more common in tropical tanks than outdoor pools. The White Spot parasite is dependent upon hosts, so that if you can remove your livestock from the pool, hopefully the parasite will be eradicated. The affected fish are best placed in running water for a week or more, if you can rig up an aquarium under a tap. Alternatively, add ten to fifteen drops of $2\frac{1}{2}$ per cent solution of mercurochrome to every ten litres of still water.

A salt bath is the answer if you find your fish suffering from leeches, easily recognized by their worm-like appearance with a disc at either end, and by their length: up to 2.5 cm. Begin with four teaspoonfuls of salt (sea salt is best if obtainable) dissolved in every ten litres of water, and increase the amount of salt daily unless the fish shows signs of distress. This is also the stock treatment for the more serious problem of fungus (although your aquarist can supply a fancy range of chemicals for this, as for many fish ailments. Some chemicals, however, may tend to make your fish infertile). The fungus *Saprolegnia ferox* is normally present in water, but fish are unlikely to become infected with it unless they are wounded in some way or are in a poor state of health. Overfed fish are less resistant to infection than those properly fed. The infection is visible as greyish-white strands, or as if cotton wool was adhering to the fish. As well as the salt bath, which should be changed daily, the affected area on the fish can be painted with diluted iodine.

Constipation should not be a problem with outdoor fish which have a varied diet. When it occurs the symptoms are sluggishness and the excrement is lengthy and knotted. Hard and dry foodstuffs and overfeeding are often the cause. Fish may right themselves, but you can transfer them for twenty-four hours to a tank containing Epsom salts at the rate of six tablespoonfuls to every six litres of water. Dried foods should be avoided for a while and chopped earthworms substituted.

For dropsy, evident by the manner in which the scales of the fish stand out and the general puffy appearance of the fish, there is no known cure. Similarly, fish whose sense of balance has been affected are usually best destroyed. One can try placing the fish in a tank heated to about 20-22°C., feeding it on earthworms and trying Epsom salts, but the results are rarely successful. Despite the long list of ailments and parasites to which fish can

fall victim, one can expect few casualties among fish living in an unpolluted, well oxygenated pond. For those who require them there are a large number of patent medicines for fish held by aquatic specialists, but as with humans so with fish: prevention is better than cure.

A problem of which I have been the unwitting cause is worth mentioning, for many pond owners must be in the same position. No text book of which I know warns against it. That is the danger of removing fish, and not only small ones, when removing clumps of overgrown weed. If you grow *Elodea*, for example, fish can easily lurk unseen in this weed and when a large number of strands are drawn up in a bunch, a fish trapped in the middle is quite powerless to make his presence known. Having transferred sizeable clumps of weed to tanks I have, on occasion, been surprised to find a fish or two swimming round in the tank a few days later. Their fate would have been quite different had the weed been intended for the rubbish dump. So do examine your surplus weed with care.

Finally, let me end this chapter by mentioning the greatest pitfall of all in owning a pond, the problem I mentioned in the first page of the book. Any depth of water is a hazard to children. Nothing attracts the young in a garden more than a pond. And nothing in a garden are they more likely to enjoy. But toddlers are only compatible with ponds if under supervision.

140

10 DIARY OF A WATER GARDEN

Memories telescope the years for all of us. So they do for me at this moment. In my mind's eye I can see quite clearly a student alternately looking at his books strewn across a table, and gazing out of the window on to a bare stretch of lawn. The room is cast in shadow and to me, the student, tired of my books, it seems dank and tiresome. Outside the autumn sun warms a crisp morning in September. It is a morning to be out and about; and the desire to be out and about is never stronger than when one has to be inside, spending long hours in studious silence. At such a time the mind grows vacant, and in being vacant, susceptible to unsought ideas.

And it was then, quite suddenly, that the idea of building a pond sprang upon me. Perhaps the bareness of the lawn or my restiveness was the cause. I cannot tell. But the vision of a pond, stocked with agile fish, well planted with colourful aquatics and marginal plants, was there before me with an irresistible clarity. The garden, it was obvious, would be transformed. But little could I have guessed the extent to which the pond would affect me, becoming, in fact, close on a daily preoccupation. Entries taken from an old diary tell the tale:

January 6 Rose as usual at 7.15 a.m. and pulled back the curtains to gaze at the pond. That has been my habit for two years or more, since the pond was built. And I do not believe it has ever looked exactly the same twice, not only because I have been constantly adding plants and hopefully making improvements, but also because nature never really pauses, even in winter. Growth, decay and change are always present. These mornings darkness obscures all but the outline of the rockery around the pond, the pond's edge and the sheet of water, and the silhouette of one or two of the taller marginals. The *Typha* dominate the scene, still tall and stately despite the ravages of winter. I have *Typha latifolia* planted in a pocket on the left-hand side and *Typha angustifolia* in a sort of shallow bay on the right. Unless it is lashing rain, after breakfast, I cross the lawn and the little bridge over the pond to enter the garage. I could, if I wished, go out the front door and reach the garage along the pavement. But that would mean I could not pause at the pond's edge. This morning there is a heavy dew and I begin the day with wet shoes. Myriads of dewdrops cling to what remains of the Sweet Galingale, most of which — too much — was cut for indoor decoration last autumn, and there are drops too on what remains of the sad, drooping leaves of the Marsh Marigold. But they will soon pick up in the coming months. A spider who has spun his web in the cleft of a Japanese Maple on the rockery has received overnight a thousand dewdrops. I wonder if he finds the result as spectacularly beautiful as we do. Probably not, all that extra weight and moisture may be to him a great nuisance. And what fly or insect would be so silly as to fly headlong into something so conspicuous?

January 9 Watching the sun just touch the edge at one side of the pond this morning, a thought suddenly occurred to me. The pond is divided into two large halves, one quite deep and the other shallow, and joined by a narrow channel over which runs the bridge.

It is the shallow half that receives the sun first and loses it last. Had I designed the pond so that the deeper half received the sun first and last, it would warm up more quickly and the deep water lilies would flower just that little bit earlier. If we were to do everything twice how perfect the world might be.

January 24 The advance of the month and the fact that I rose a little later than usual, meant that the rising sun had quite covered half of the pond before I pulled my curtains. I hastened out to the bridge before breakfast. The air was sharp and utterly still, the sky lightly ribbed with white and red-streaked clouds. The water provided a perfect mirror image, broken only by one of the rubber balls which had stuck fast to a leaf of Water Hawthorn. A single goldfish, one of the larger ones, cruises slowly round in the deepest part. He is presumably looking for food, but is in no great need of it. The rest of the fish that I have left outdoors are either completely hidden in the dense foliage of *Elodea* or are but partly visible. I can pick out the odd streak of gold here and there, the back or tail of a goldfish or Shubunkin. A morning like this, the clearness and stillness makes one expectant of spring, but the weather is unlikely to remain so calm for long. I dally at the pond's edge visualizing the growth to come and return indoors to hard toast and lukewarm coffee.

January 27 The weather forecast on the radio this morning blithely declared that snow could be expected in the north of the country. That was reason enough to expect snow here in the south. Sure enough by evening the first of the snow arrived. I stood on the bridge watching the flakes fall soundlessly into the water, disappearing into the depths for ever. On the rockery a few flakes perched temporarily on the heather and junipers, but only on the rocks did the snow remain. In the fading light the pond looked gaunt and old.

January 28 It has snowed during the night and the whole garden is blanketed. What a contrast to last night when the rockery looked so patchy. The pond, however, has not frozen and looks like an ugly black gash in the pure white landscape. I do not want to spoil this pristine sight by marking the snow with footprints, but Cliff (our young Jack Russell terrier) is soon haring round the garden, sending up great flurries of snow in his wake. I watch his joy for several minutes until he turns to the rockery. The thought of crocuses making their way up only to be churned out of the ground makes me roar at him. He returns to the house very crestfallen.

February 1 The temperature has dropped several degrees over the last few days and more snow has fallen. The junipers, especially *Juniperus sabina* 'Blue Danube' with its overlapping branches pointing slightly upwards, spread out with their white coverings and occasional markings of dark green, look extraordinarily impressive. I gingerly try walking on the pond and to my delight find that it bears my weight. There is no need to keep a hole open for the fish. I am confident that the depth of the pool and the fact that there is very little decaying matter on the bottom means the oxygen level of the water will remain high and the toxic gases low. Beneath the ice I can make out the shapes of fish quite clearly. The Golden Orfe, in particular, seem to be on the move. Is it the vibration of my footsteps that has them agitated? As I move about they scurry away to left and right. When I tread more softly they remain still longer, but are still reluctant to allow me to pass right over them. A slight tapping of my heel makes them dart about in agitation. Fish are highly sensitive to vibration.

February 3 The temperature has risen again. I find out the hard way. Took a whim to skate over the ice on the way to the garage this morning. The ice cracked at the shallow end which gets the early sun. Returned to the house to change socks, shoes and trousers. In the afternoon, Peter came in from next door on some pretext and headed straight for the pond. I warned him to no avail. The ice held for him at the deep end. I then, maliciously, threw some coins near the spot where I went in. To my secret disappointment, that bore his light weight and he went off with a handsome profit.

February 7 The snow has turned to slush and the garden looks miserable. The plants on the rockery are sodden and downcast. The innumerable small stones and pebbles seem to have emerged from the muddy soil giving the rockery an unpleasant gravelly appearance. I suppose this is caused by the soil sinking with the weight of melting ice and snow. Once the soil has dried out sufficiently I will rake it well over.

February 26 What stamina crocuses possess. They were out today in the midst of radiant sunshine, and it must be a month or more since they first appeared. (Pity that the leaves give the rockery a slightly tatty appearance once the flowers are finally over.) But they make a pretty, welcoming appearance at this time of year in conjunction with Winter Aconite, *Chinodoxa, Scilla, Gallanthus* and the two early heathers I have planted, *Erica* 'Springwood White' and *carnea*. Planted in dense clumps these little bulbs do much to remove the bleakness of the pond during the winter months. I notice that a few of the crocuses have had trouble showing above the branches of the prostrate junipers and heathers. This is indicative of how rapidly these evergreen plants can grow in a few seasons.

When planting the bulbs I put them in well clear of the junipers' spreading branches.

March 7 Spring has now truly arrived at the pond. For the last few days *Rhododendron praecox* with their delicate but rich shade of violet flowers have been in full bloom. Bulbs, even when flowering in quantity, do no more than contribute colouring to their surroundings. These rhododendrons are really magnificent plants; though not much more than a metre high, any of them, they all dominate their surroundings. The whole area around the pond seems to be filled with colour while the *praecox* lasts. They begin a firmer shade of violet than they end. In the sunshine the trumpet flowers appear quite pale and light. But when viewed in the fading light of a March afternoon, their colour becomes altogether richer, the flowers almost seeming to emit their own light. While everything else around the pond (bulbs apart) begins to disappear into the dusk, the rhododendrons remain conspicuous and brilliant right into the end of the day. I can think of few pleasures to equal standing by the pool in the half light of a March evening admiring these gorgeous plants, hearing an occasional gurgle as a goldfish rises to the surface, seeing the purplish ripples gently cross the pool and stop; and then become aware of utter silence returning again. Fed the fish for the first time this year, just a few flakes. Felt cold after being by the pool for some time, so returned to the house to curl up by the fire with a book and a glass of port.

March 22 Hard frost and bitter East winds have alternated with each other over the past weeks. The rhododendrons are now on the wane. Indeed of the seven plants I possess, three have now lost their blooms entirely. They are, without exception, those situated where the morning sun reaches them before the frost has melted off their blooms. This shortens the life of the blooms to a marked degree. Having been out of the house all day, I looked forward to spending a few minutes by the pond before supper. But the wind swung into the West during the afternoon to bring rain. As I write this now it is simply lashing out of the heavens as the radio forecast warned at breakfast time. I did not believe a word of it.

March 23   Having read late into the night, I woke up more sleepily than usual and stared sightlessly out on the damp morning. Then a sight half-hidden by a boulder woke me up with a start. I could just make out the grey, thin form of a heron. So well did his colour merge with the surrounding soil and rockery that I doubt if I should have noticed him but for the slight jerk he made as I pulled back the curtains. I immediately banged the window. He cocked his head to one side, and then flew off on those great ponderous wings. I dressed as quickly as possible and rushed down to the pond to count the fish. The weed is too dense to be absolutely certain of counting them all. I poked round with a long stick. It is amazing how well the fish recognize danger. Normally, if I were to run a stick or net through the weeds, the fish would simply swim off to a quieter spot; but now they try to bury themselves into the bottom of the pond as far out of sight as possible. I counted only eight Golden Orfe and there should be fifteen. Two goldfish and one Shubunkin appear to be missing too. I do not know why the Golden Orfe should suffer the largest number of casualties. Just as I was returning to the house in disgust I spotted a goldfish half over on its side nearly hidden by a rock near the bottom of the waterfall. Closer inspection revealed that it had a nasty wound along one flank and a cut across the back. The heron was probably about to gorge the fish when I disturbed him and dropped it in his haste. Of course it happens to be the tamest of all my goldfish.

All last summer I fed him on worms and morsels direct from my fingers. He was, I suppose, the most vulnerable by being the least shy. I blame myself for not covering the pond. Netting the fish as gently as I could, I brought him indoors to a mild salt bath. I would not be optimistic about his chances, however. I had breakfast by the window, and not quarter of an hour after I had frightened the heron off, I saw him return and circle round before I ran into the garden. Doubtless the heavy rain last night has coloured the local rivers and food is scarce. I am determined to build an arched wall right round the pond and stretch a net overhead. It is the only answer.

March 27   The daffodils are out in all their colourfulness now, but I made a mistake in planting them on the rockery at all. They are too tall and out of proportion to the rest of the plants. A few miniature narcissi would look much happier situated beside the little maples and under the willow. When the trees have grown larger there will be time enough for the larger daffodils. John B., an enthusiastic gardener, came over in the late afternoon. He asked me if I had both the single and double forms of Marsh Marigold. I pointed out the two plants, remarking that I expected the single to flower first. No, he countered, the double always comes out first. I distinctly remembered the single coming out first last year and told him so. But he remained adamant, so it remains to be seen. The sick fish has not developed fungus infection in his wound, but he looks very low in the aquarium where I have placed him, lying on the bottom breathing heavily and with effort.

April 2   I am right. Two flowers of the single Marsh Marigold opened today, later than last year but still ahead of the double variety. I rang John in glee. He is nonplussed and simply replied that none of his is out yet.

Crossing the bridge this morning I did a 'double take' in suddenly noticing that the lilies have moved, a number of red leaf shoots were quite apparent. The recent mild spell has evidently warmed up the pool and stirred the lilies into life. The sick fish showed very little sign of life or movement in the aquarium before I left the house. He had keeled over slightly to one side. This evening, on my return, he was on the surface, dead.

April 7 The frogs have left their hidey-holes in force over the last few days and are now happily mating in the pond. There must be thirty or more pairs. How such small bodies can produce such a mass of spawn is difficult to understand. It is spread over more than a metre. My mind goes back to the school pond. At morning break, as schoolboys, we would rush to the pond's edge in spring to watch scores of frogs frantically joined in copulation. If a master appeared we would back away from the pond, sheepishly. I doubt if today's school children would be so coy. I have heard it said that a bullfrog, in his enthusiasm, is capable of mounting a fish by mistake and strangling it to death. I very much doubt if that is possible and certainly have never seen it happen. The frogs invariably lay their spawn in the shallowest part of the pond, presumably because it is warmer. Difference of temperature may also explain why frogs emerge to mate at widely different times even in a comparatively small locality. The same reason could hardly explain why John's double Marsh Marigold came out before his single, whereas the opposite was true for me. He rang me triumphantly this evening. 'We're quits,' he announced.

April 11 Simon R. bought me round a small tuber of *Nymphaea* 'Laydekeri Purpurata', which he had promised me last year. I thanked him profusely and mumbled something about hoping he had not lifted it too

early in the year. There is still comparatively little growth in the pond. The Water Hawthorn has reached the surface but none of the water lilies has, and the water is still chilly. I wished Simon had waited another fortnight or more when all the plants would be on the move. I visited David yesterday to admire his *Orontium*. What a fine specimen it is. He has it planted in more than half a metre of water, nearer three-quarters I would say, and the leaves float on the surface while the white and yellow flowers emerge from the water quite erect. I have been promised a piece later.

April 21 I had the luck to have to take the three-hour train journey from Dublin to Cork today, I got to the station early to be certain of a window seat. As I had anticipated, all along the canals, along practically every river and rivulet, pond and lake, there was an abundance of Marsh Marigold. The strength of that yellow is nothing if not extraordinary. Wherever the plant is to be found it radiates a brilliant warmth, be it in ditch, on river bank or moist meadow. While the rest of the carriage carried on an inane conversation about some football controversy, I happily whiled away the hours with my nose pressed up against the window pane like a child. Of the several hundred passengers aboard, I do not suppose more than half a dozen actually took the trouble to notice these lovely plants or the Bog Bean (though far less obvious at a distance). And I daresay many a confirmed gardener might pass them by too, and for no other reason than the plants are neither rare nor come from foreign shores. No man is a prophet ... as they say, and no plant either. I returned home about seven, by which time the light breeze had cooled and taken on that unmistakable tang of new growth. It was sheer ecstasy. As the sun sank I pondered over the day's work seated on a rock by the pond, breathing in the air and admiring still the humble Marsh Marigold. Actually, its other name, King Cup, describes it more appropriately. Like the *praecox*, the dimming light seems only to heighten its brilliance.

April 27 The two or three sprigs of Bog Bean that I collected two years ago have filled one corner of the pond, and the superb little flowers are now at their peak of beauty. The Bog Bean is abundant throughout the wetlands and it is strange to think that a thousand cows must daily have the privilege of crushing into the mud one of the most exquisite of all water-loving plants. Happily, the Bog Bean can well take such treatment.

April 29 The recent spell of sunny weather has given the water a slight cloudy tinge. It will only be temporary. The tips of the *elodeas* are now a vivid light green — a sign of growth — and they will clear the pond in no time.

May 4 As if by magic the water was crystal clear this morning, whereas only yesterday it was less than perfect. I examined Simon's lily 'Laydekeri Purpurata': it had sent up no shoots and on lifting it I discovered the tuber had begun to rot. I know what I should have done: placed it in the greenhouse in a shallow bowl. The magpies may not have helped. Having put the lily basket in shallow water, the birds paddled in the mud probably with a view to catching tadpoles which are wriggling round in their thousands, but also damaging any young shoots that may possibly have appeared. I spotted a Common Newt seemingly nibbling at a piece of *Potamogeton crispus*. He saw me too and fled into a clump of *Myriophyllum*. I presume there must be more newts about and that they have entered the pond to mate. But I have seen only one batch of their eggs, laid out like a string of pearls.

May 7 Finding that the writing was going badly, I sauntered down to the pond for a short break. Predictably the short break turned

into something longer. I became engrossed in watching a small hatch of Mayfly *(Emphemera danica)* brought on by the recent warm weather. The nymphs were rising, struggling to the surface, anxiously kicking and fighting their way out of their penultimate coats to become duns; then flying, none too skilfully, to trees, bushes and marginals (where I lost sight of them) to moult again and become, if only for a day, graceful hovering spinners. Quite why these insects should be called Mayfly is something of a mystery. The largest hatches nearly always take place in June and sometimes there are none at all in May. Could it have anything to do with the change of the calendar?

May 10 The pond is now, for the first time this year, a mass of colour. Aubretia and phlox in purple, red and white, colour the rockery. In the bog garden the little *Calla palustris* or Bog Arum is fully out as are the *Lysichitum americanun* plants in the opposite corner. *Ranunculus aconitifolius*, the White Bachelor's Buttons, is blossoming (it needs to be cleared of weeds that have sprung up around it), and the *Primula pulverulenta* are about to burst forth. The Marsh Marigold is far from over, the double is just about at its height, and behind all, though creeping forward somewhat, is the lovely *Polygonum bistort*. In the pond itself, the Water Crowfoot is producing its little white flowers, the small leaves of the *Villarsia* 'Bennettii' or Water Fringe are beginning to dot the surface and the Water Hawthorn has several blossoms fully open. And the Water Gladiole, Tongue Buttercup and the reeds are all shooting skywards.

May 15 The electrician came to repair the electric cable to the pond. It was a new man and I brought him down the garden to show him where the cable was laid. He stood looking around at the pond and the rockery for a few moments and then said: 'Where did you get all those rocks from?' That is always the first question anyone who has no interest in gardening asks. The second is where did you buy all those fish? Sure enough our new electrician asked me that too.

May 17 We had invited a few friends in for drinks and got a superb morning for it. Sitting, walking and talking around the pond we whiled away a few hours in as pleasant a way as I think possible. All I missed was the tinkling of the waterfall which I have yet to connect to the new cable.

May 20 I went round to David to obtain a root of his Golden Club which he promised to divide. He put on a hefty pair of waders and entered the pond, actually it is more like a lake. After ten minutes he had become truly stuck in the mud without having had any success in dividing the plant. I gave him the handle of a rake to extricate him, and after much pulling and heaving he managed to get back to the shore. The roots of *Orontium aquaticum* are very tenacious. Needless to say I went home without the plant.

May 29 Since we use a great deal of water mint with our potatoes I decided to add to our stock of plants, which before summer's end are usually denuded of leaves. I strolled down the bank of the local stream, through the meadow and on through two more fields as far as the swamp and I found only one meagre plant at the very end. I could have sworn all along the bank there were clumps of the plant last year. On the return journey, I walked through the fields at a distance of about five or six metres from the stream. I suddenly came across an abundance of water mint partially concealed in the long grass. It is curious that it should not be growing at the water's edge but in the drier - though still moist - soil some distance away. It only goes to show how often a plant will thrive in one particular place - not always the most obvious one - and make no headway a few metres to left or right.

June 4 All the water-lilies now have several flower buds each. The earliest to actually flower was 'Marliacea Chromatella' which opened briefly just before midday yesterday. The wind turned to the East immediately after lunch and the bloom closed again like a clam. One would expect *Nymphaea alba* to be the first to bloom since it is the native lily, used to our moderate temperatures, but it will be several days yet before its first bud even breaks the surface. 'James Brydon' is likely to be the last to bloom as the buds are still close to the crown. But this lily is well worth waiting for, not only on account of the beauty of the flower, but also because it throws up so many in proportion to the number of leaves.

June 6 The first flower of 'Chromatella' has now sunk back. How short a time they last, but it has beem replaced by two further blooms. 'Escarboucle' has one small bloom out too. It is slightly tinged with white, so I presume it comes from a young tuber off the mainstock. I must say the blotched appearance of young 'Escarboucle' blooms look almost like a disease, they remind me of alopecia. However, one has no choice but to wait for the plant to mature. John was on the phone to enquire if any of my lilies were out. I said my first came out four days ago. He immediately retorted that all his plants had been in flower a fortnight ago. I know how he does it. He lays a sheet of polythene over the pond in early spring. It has the same effect as a glass-house. I should dislike the sight of polythene straddling the pond while the rockery is so colourful and should you get a late frost after removing the polythene, all that accelerated growth would have been for nothing.

June 19 Every time I cross the bridge and look to left and right, I am irritated by the fact that the water level in the right-hand part appears lower than in the left. The reason is, of course, that proper account was not taken of the level of the ground when the pond was dug out. The difference is very slight but still annoying. However, the Brooklime has all but concealed the bare concrete. It is a vigorous plant and I like the shiny, wax-like green leaves, but the tiny blue flowers are too small to provide much colour. I might think of substituting something else.

June 26 If I were to choose one day out of the year as showing the pond in its absolute prime, then this would be the one. I counted twenty-one lilies in full bloom this morning: four *alba*; four 'Froebeli'; three 'James Brydon'; five 'Chromatella'; three 'Escarboucle' (all pure red) and two 'Moorei'. The irises are resplendent too. *Iris pseudacorus* still has a few blooms and a few buds left; *laevigata* is just about at its height and *sibirica* is flowering more profusely than even last year. I have the Irises grouped round the pond in pockets about one and a half metres long at a stretch. This spreads the colour over the whole area. The Tongue Buttercup is now in flower too and will provide colour from now until early autumn. And the variegated foliage of *Acorus, Scirpus tabernaemontani zebrinus* and *Glyceria* will make a striking display until the end of summer and indeed well into the autumn.

June 28 It is amusing how a plant will surreptitiously move itself from a position it does not like to a more congenial one. I put in a few young shoots of *Myosotis* in the damp soil close to the *Typha angustifolia*. Now after a few seasons it has spread round behind the *Typha*, presumably to avail of the cool, moist shade the tall leaves of the bulrush provide.

June 29 This was an afternoon to which I had been looking forward: afternoon tea at Rosemary's. And it could not have turned out more perfectly, for it was a sultry, cloudless day with not a breeze to disturb as much as a leaf. We walked the garden up and down, examining each plant in turn. Far away could be heard the occasional hum of a car, a sound made tiny in comparison with the chuckling sparrows at the pond's edge, the crows calling lazily overhead and the busy passing sounds of many insects. In this spacious, old world garden, full of gravelled paths, sweet-smelling herbs, foxgloves, irises, poppies and columbine, lupins, climbing roses, hydrangeas, honeysuckle and buddleias, one could as well be in the depths of the country as in a town. And what could be a more congenial setting for sipping afternoon tea? We sat, as always, by the pond, and discussed a thousand questions on lilies and marginals, which plants to thin back, which plants to divide and share. The sun was glinting through the poplars as I walked home, full of hot buttered scones, chocolate cake — and a warm feeling of wellbeing.

July 3 The little red flowers of Water Milfoil look very effective against the white of the Crowfoot and the occasional flower of *Elodea densa;* but perhaps too much of the surface area is covered, indeed cluttered with plants. The water-lilies have spread out a good deal and are vying for space not only with the Crowfoot and Water Hawthorn, but *Villarsia,* a very vigorous grower, and the Water Soldier which has come up to the surface in abundance. Greet, the Dutch au pair from next door, was in this evening and looking aghast said: 'You don't grow that, do you?' pointing at the *Stratiotes*. I nodded: 'Why not?' She explained that in Holland it is so prolific that it clutters up many ditches and small waterways. I said it was a rarity in this part of the world and was, in any case, a most attractive plant. She wrinkled her nose sceptically and laughed. The broad, matt colours of the *Iris kaempferi* were what appealed to her. 'They are ten a penny on the rice paddies of Japan,' I remarked. She laughed again.

July 5 I spent a pleasant afternoon wading through the pond thinning out *Elodea canadensis* which had become very bushy indeed. I do not like stirring up the pond during the height of summer but if I leave it until autumn it means removing essential winter cover. I am amazed at how unfearful the fish are at my presence. They come right up to where I am pulling out the weed, curious to see what is going on. How utterly different is their behaviour when a heron is about. How do they distinguish friend from foe? They must have some means of relaying danger one to the other, but I am not aware of any research into this. Out of interest, I placed a few handfuls of *Elodea* in the empty aquarium along with a few scoopings of mud, just to see what insect life they contain. The pond was quite coloured by the time I had finished the job, but by leaving the waterfall running it had begun to clear perceptibly within four or five hours and will be back to its usual state in a matter of days.

July 7 I examined the aquarium since it had cleared and discovered quite a variety of life. I found: a Water Scorpion, a Great Diving Beetle (pretty sick I would think, not much movement out of him), a Water Boatman and a dead Pond Skater. There were numerous shrimps and a Caddis Fly larva, I think *Limnephilus flavicornis*, which seemed to be attempting to add to its cumbersome shell by playing around with a tiny stone. There were also a number of blood worms, *Tubifex*, waving their thin, bright red bodies around for all they were worth and I glimpsed a leech, wriggling its way through the water at speed.

July 12 Time loses its meaning in July. One can just lie at the pond's edge watching the great rolling clouds drift into and out of the water, follow the Golden Orfe and goldfish and Shubunkins on their endless travels through the weeds; and gaze thoughtlessly at the lily blooms, the bright colours of the Monkey Flower, red, yellow and orange; and one can listen to the whispering of the wind through Reed Mace, Bulrush and Galingale. On such a day as today, the worries of the world recede and lose their meaning.

July 16 We have been exceptionally lucky with the weather this month. I cannot remember for how many consecutive days now we have had supper at the edge of the pool. And once the table is put out the fish immediately swim over to share whatever titbits we throw in. Since we usually have a salad, there is hard-boiled egg, well chopped, to spare.

July 23 While visiting a nearby public garden this afternoon, I noticed they had obtained a fine mass of *Cotula coronopifolia*, Brass Buttons. I immediately thought of where this low growing, dense plant could fit into the scheme of my own pond. I approached a gardener and to my joy found that he could not identify the plant. Would he mind if I took a small piece away to have it identified? Not at all, so with his imprimatur I was able to march past the official at the gate with impunity. It was a neat variation on the 'tie your shoe lace' subterfuge. Where the *Veronica beccabunga* currently conceals the cement edge I shall plant the *Cotula*; it is more colourful.

July 26 Today I noticed more honey bees than usual crawling around the edge of the pond or alighting on lily leaves. This is a sure sign that the honey flow in the area is over.

149

The nectar bees collect from flowers contains a high percentage of moisture. When nectar is scarce, the bees supplement their water supply by visiting the pond.

July 27 Despite the high winds, I visited Mount Usher in Ashford this morning. I need not have worried. The winds, so far from detracting from the ferns, added to them. I walked through the fernery and I experienced something quite different from their usual tranquility in watching their fronds flash dramatically forward and backwards. My favourite display of Astilbes are to be found at Mount Usher. There the plants are grouped all around the bog gardens, around which one can walk on numerous paths. The shrubs and trees conceal one area from another; and every new area that you enter has its own set of surprises, its own style.

August 1 The last month of summer, and the most opulent one. But even in the midst of opulence there are signs of decay. All the water lilies have yellow and frayed leaves. I have tried to cut them off and remove them, also some of the green leaves, so that the ratio of leaves to flowers is improved. The Japanese Arrowhead is about to flower and so is the *Alisma* and Bog Cotton. *Sagittaria* always seems to fascinate children. Padraig and Niamh were in before supper. Padraig fingered the top of an Arrowhead leaf to see if it was sharp. Then he asked why it was standing in water. 'So it can drink,' I replied; 'We all have to do that to survive.' 'But what about the plants that are not in the water?' he queried. I could see I was in for a question-and-answer session. 'They are able to take water from the soil too, it is just that on the bank there is less moisture.' He paused for a moment and I thought his mind had moved elsewhere. Then he asked, 'How do they drink water?' I picked an Arrowhead leaf, held it up to the light and pointed out

the veins. 'There,' I said, 'the leaf uses all those veins just the way you use a drinking straw.' I have rarely seen such a sense of wonder enter a child's eyes. 'All leaves are a bit like that,' I added, and he marched off round the garden picking leaves and holding them up to the light.

August 10 The sense of balance that I had achieved by planting *Typha angustifolia* at one end of the pond and *latifolia* at the other has come undone, since *latifolia* has left its neat pocket and taken large strides across the pond. Once the pokers have matured in September when they can be cut for indoor decoration, I intend cutting out the plant entirely and replacing it with *Typha minima*. That will restore the balance permanently.

August 18 Gazing into the pool near the bridge I suddenly spotted a fish no more than a centimetre long. I had never seen it before, and closer inspection of the water revealed a number of minute fish, no thicker than the stem of a pin. Presumably, they have hatched quite recently.

August 26 Returned from a weekend in Paris at 3. a.m., having had to land at Cork and take a train up. I should have been home at 4 p.m. yesterday, but heavy fog over the whole country delayed departure by some ten hours. The tedious wait was more than worthwhile. I shall not easily forget the sight of the pond through that heavy morning mist. The bulrushes looked weird with their pokers emerging at intervals through the vague light. The prostrate junipers stretched out unmoving branches, dripping at the water's edge. Their character seemed quite changed by the fog, eerie, and yet splendid in a strange way. From the water, the *Alisma* flower stems rose like new-fangled aerials, and the lily pads seemed to be floating on nothing, or like clouds suspended in time and air. There was no sound, except an occasional dripping of water off leaves, or the plop of a frog disappearing into the pond for safety. The garden was full of them, I counted fifteen before giving up, picking my way gingerly between them, across the bridge, over the lawn and so to bed.

September 3 What stamina the *Mimulus, Myosotis* and *Veronica beccabunga* possess. This will be their third month in flower. True, the *beccabunga* is almost over and the Myosotis is throwing up fewer blooms, but I expect the *Mimulus* to continue to flower until the first frosts, maybe even a little after. The *Pontederia* is in full bloom.

September 10 There is an autumn stillness over the pond now, almost a hushed quietness. The earth is beginning to smell raw again with heavy dews. The pokers of the bulrushes have turned a rich brown and the Water Fringe is flowering yet; the Pickerel Weed, *Mimulus* and the foliage of the Manna Grass, which is obtaining its autumn tint along with the maples, are the main centres of attraction, with the water lilies of course. We savour the last few days reminiscent of summer warmth, having morning coffee by the pool when at home. The fish have become less agile; with the dropping of the temperature they move more slowly and spend longer amongst the weeds.

September 25 Faithful to the last, 'Froebeli' is still flowering profusely. There were three blooms this afternoon. 'Chromatella' produced one as did 'Escarboucle' yesterday. It is interesting to note how much longer the blooms remain open in autumn, right up till late afternoon. In summer the flowers are much more sensitive to changes in temperature. This is especially true if the temperature is exceptionally high in the morning. Once it drops in the afternoon, be it only a few

degrees, the flowers quickly close up. Now, in late September, the flowers remain open for hours, impervious to the chilling wind.

October 3 The first frosts are upon us. The season of the pond is now over. I have little to do but clear away the dead leaves and snip off most of those still green. There is hardly any point in leaving them now. The next fine day I shall cut back the leaves of the marginals. It is slightly sad to see the end of growth and the pond bereft of all its summer flowers. But so it must be until another year. One important job still remains. The brick wall is now complete except for the two arches through which to enter and leave the pond. Once they are up I shall net over the water garden. This winter the fish will be safe.

Such entries as these could be the lot of any gardener. Of no significance to the world at large, they are none the worse for that. For it is through what we create or with what we live, day by day, that gives our lives most meaning. As events, thoughts and people crowd through my memory, I am aware that some of my happiest moments have been spent in the water garden. It has been an integral part of much that I have most enjoyed. On the keystone in one of the arches put up many years ago, was inscribed the saying: *'Sursum Corda'* — Lift up Your Hearts; be of Good Cheer. That is what water gardening has meant to me. And so I hope it will be for you.

Appendix I: Useful Figures and Conversions

10 mm.	=	⅜ inch
2.54 cm.	=	1 inch
30 cm.	=	12 inches
1 metre	=	3 feet 3 inches
1 sq. metre	=	1.2 sq. yards (10.75 sq. feet)
1 cubic metre (1000 litres)	=	1.3 cubic yards (35.3 cubic feet)
4.54 litres	=	1 Imp. gallon
3.79 litres	=	1 US gallon
1 cubic metre	=	220 Imp. gallons or 263.9 US gallons
1 kilogram	=	2.2 lb
50 kg.	=	1 cwt.

I Imp. gallon of water weighs 10 lb
1 US gallon of water weighs 8.3 lb
1 cubic metre of water = 1000 kilograms

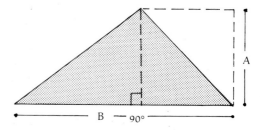

Surface area = ½A × B

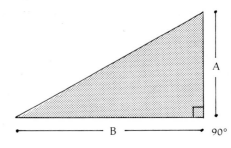

Surface area = ½A × B

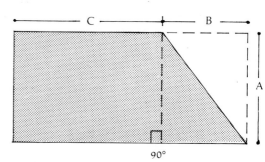

Surface area = A × C + ½A × B

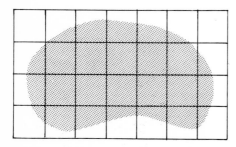

To estimate surface area of an irregular pond Divide area into squares and average out the fractions. This is a useful method of determining the amount of concrete required for the base of a pond. (The surface area is, of course, multiplied by the thickness of the concrete to give you the quantity.)

To measure the surface area and circumference of a circular pond

Area of circle = πr^2
Circumference of circle = $2\pi r$
($\pi = 3.14159$)

To estimate the surface area of a triangular pond It sometimes happens that a triangular pond will suit a particular part of a patio better than any other shape. This is particularly true if you have a wall meeting the patio at a sharp angle.

The area of the circle multiplied by the thickness of the concrete will equal the amount of concrete required for the base. The circumference of the circle multiplied by the depth of the pond, and the result multiplied by the thickness of the concrete will provide an estimate of the concrete required for the wall. (The estimate will be marginally on the high side.) To inscribe a circle, drive a stake into the centre of the ground. Attach to the stake a rope which should be the length of the radius of the circle. At the other end of the rope attach a sharp point (a piece of sharp wood or a heavy nail will serve the purpose). Use this to inscribe the circumference.

Polygon ponds If you want to make a regular, many-sided pond, begin by inscribing a circle whose diameter represents the maximum width of the pond. Then divide 360° by the number of sides the pond is to have. Let us say it is to be a six-sided pond. Then 360° ÷ 6 = 60°. Draw one line from the centre of the circle to the circumference i.e. one radius. Then draw a second radius at an angle of 60° to the first, then draw a third at 60° to the second and so on until six radii are drawn. (Alternatively, one could simply draw three diameters at equal intervals in this instance. This would not be possible with a seven-sided figure, for example.) Join up the six radii where they meet the circumference and the result is a hexagon. Treat as so many triangles to determine the amount of concrete required for the base.

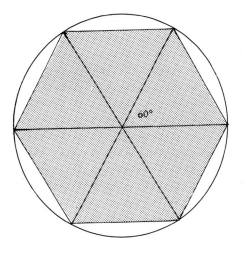

An oval pond can be made by driving two stakes into the ground and attaching a rope to them. The area inscribed by the rope will be an oval. Treat as an irregular pond to determine the surface area.

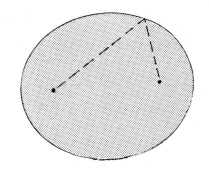

Rectangular ponds Are the dimensions of one rectangular pond more pleasing than another? The Greeks certainly thought so. Bisect one side of a square and join the mid-point to one of the opposite corners. Using this line as a radius, inscribe part of a circle to meet the extended side of the square. The resulting rectangle will have sides in the ratio 1 : 1.618; and such a rectangle is often regarded as of ideal proportions.

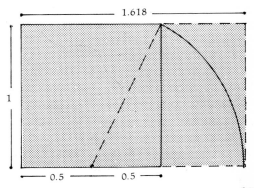

Appendix II: Marginal and Bog Plants

The heights of plants vary a great deal according to the conditions under which they are grown. The heights given below are those which the plant might be expected to attain under favourable conditions. DS stands for damp soil, WS for wet soil; and an entry such as DS - 6 cm. means the plant will succeed in any conditions from damp soil to 6 cm. of water over its crown. * = Tender plants.

LATIN NAME	COMMON NAME	HEIGHT	HABITAT	SEASON
Acorus calamus	Sweet Flag	60-90 cm.	WS - 5 cm.	summer
A. calamus 'Variegatus'		60-90 cm.	WS - 4 cm.	summer
A. gramineus		30 cm.	WS - 4 cm.	summer
Alisma lanceolatum	Water Plantain	30-45 cm.	WS - 20 cm.	mid-late summer
A. plantago-aquatica	Great Water Plantain	30-90 cm.	WS - 25 cm.	mid-late summer
Aruncus sylvester	Goat's Beard	1.3 m.	DS - WS	summer
A. kneiffi		60 cm.	DS - WS	summer
Astilbe arendsii		60 cm. - 1.8 m.	DS - WS	summer
A. simplicifolia		22 cm.	DS - WS	summer
Butomus umbellatus	Flowering Rush	1 m.	up to 10 cm.	summer
Calla palustris	Bog Arum	25 cm.	WS - 6 cm.	summer
Caltha palustris	King Cup, Marsh Marigold	30 cm.	WS - 6 cm.	early spring
C. palustris alba		15-20 cm.	WS - 6 cm.	early spring
C. palustris flore-pleno		25 cm.	WS - 6 cm.	early spring
C. polypetala		60-90 cm.	WS - 6 cm.	early spring
*Canna hybrids	Canna lily/Water Canna	1.2 m.	DS - 15 cm.	summer
Carex pendula		1-1.3 m.	DS - WS	
C. riparia 'Bowles' Golden'		45 cm.	WS - 6 cm.	
C. stricta		1-1.3 m.	DS - WS	
*Colcasia esculenta	Green Taro	1.1 m.	WS - 30 cm.	summer
*C. esculenta fontanesii	Red Stemmed Taro	1.1 m.	WS - 30 cm.	summer
Cortaderia argentea	Pampas Grass	2 m.	DS	late sum/aut
C. quila	Pampas Grass	2 m.	DS	late sum/aut
Cotula coronopifolia	Brass Buttons	25 cm.	WS - 6 cm.	summer
Cyperus alternifolius	Umbrella Grass	90 cm.	WS - 6 cm.	late summer
C. longus	Sweet Galingale	60 cm.-1.1 m.	DS - 6 cm.	late summer
*Cyperus haspans	Papyrus	45 cm.	WS - 15 cm.	summer
Eriophorum angustifolium	Cotton Grass, Bog Cotton	30 cm.	WS acid	spring-early summer
E. latifolium		40 cm.	WS acid	summer
E. vaginatum		30 cm.	WS acid	summer
Filipendula ulmaria plena	Double Meadowsweet, Spirea	90cm. - 1.5cm.	DS - WS	late summer

LATIN NAME	COMMON NAME	HEIGHT	HABITAT	SEASON
Glyceria aquatica variegata (G. spectabilis)	Manna Grass	30-90 cm.	WS - 15 cm.	summer
Gunnera manicata		2-4 m.	WS	spring
Hemerocallis	Day Lily	70 cm. - 1.2 m	DS	late summer
Hosta fortunei marginata alba	Plantain Lily	75 cm.	DS	late summer
H. glauca (sieboldiana)		60-75 cm.	DS	late summer
H. glauca fortunei (fortunei)		75 cm.	DS	late summer
H. lancifolia		60 cm.	DS	late summer
H. ventricosa		90 cm.	DS	late summer-autumn
Iris kaempferi		60-75 cm.	DS (winter) - 6 cm. (summer) acid soil	summer
Iris fulva	Red Iris	60 cm.	WS - 15 cm.	spring/variable
I. laevigata		60 cm.	WS - 10 cm.	summer
I. pseudacorus variegatus	Yellow Flag	75 cm. - 1 m.	WS - 10 cm.	summer
I. pseudacorus bastardi		75 cm. - 1 m.	WS - 10 cm.	summer
I. sibirica		90 cm.	DS - 10 cm.	summer
I. versicolor	Blue Flag	90 cm.	WS - 10 cm.	summer
*Louisiana irises named hybrids	Louisiana iris	to 1.2 m.	DS - 15 cm.	spring
Juncus effusus spiralis	Corkscrew Rush	45 cm.	WS - 6 cm.	late summer
J. ensifolius		1 m.	WS - 6 cm.	summer
Lysichitum americanum	False American Skunk Cabbage, Bog Arum	90 cm. - 1.2 m.	WS - 5 cm.	spring
L. camtschatcense		30 cm.-1 m.	WS - 6 cm.	spring
Mentha aquatica	Water Mint	30 cm.	DS - 5 cm.	late summer
Menyanthes trifoliata	Bog Bean	prostrate	WS - 10 cm.	spring
Mimulus cardinalis	Monkey Flower	35 cm.	WS	summer
M. guttatus		45 cm.	WS	summer
M. luteus		45 cm.	WS	summer
M. moschatus		12 cm.	WS	summer
M. ringens		50 cm.	WS - 5 cm.	summer
Myosotis scorpioides (palustris)	Water-Forget-Me-Not	20 cm.	WS - 5 cm.	summer
Orontium aquaticum	Golden Club	30-45 cm.	WS - 45 cm.	spring
Polygonum bistort	Knotwood	60 cm.	DS - WS	
Pontederia cordata	Pickerel Weed	45-75 cm.	to 12 cm.	late summer
P. lanceolata		1.5 m.	to 20 cm.	late summer

LATIN NAME	COMMON NAME	HEIGHT	HABITAT	SEASON
Primula beesiana		45 cm.	WS	spring
P. denticulata	Himalayan Primrose	30-45 cm.	DS	spring
P. florindae	Himalayan Cowslip	90 cm.	WS	spring
P. frondosa		15 cm.	WS	spring
P. japonica		45 cm.	WS	late spring-summer
P. pulverulenta		90 cm.	WS	summer
P. rosea		15 cm.	WS	spring
P. sikkimensis		60 cm.	WS	spring
Ranunculus aconitifolius flore-pleno	White Bachelor's Buttons Fair Maids of France	45 cm.	DS - WS	spring-early summer
R. acris flore pleno		45 cm.	DS - WS	spring-early summer
R. lingua (grandiflora)	Tongue Buttercup, Greater Spearwort	60-90 cm.	WS - 6 cm.	summer
Rheum inopinatum	Rhubarb	60 cm.	WS	late spring
R. palmatum atrosanguineum		2.5 m.	WS·	late spring
Rodgersia pinnata alba		60 cm.	DS	late summer
R. pinnata elegans		60 cm.	DS	late summer
Sagittaria japonica/flore pleno	Japanese Arrowhead	75 cm.	to 15 cm.	late summer
S. sagittifolia	Common Arrowhead	50 cm.	to 15 cm.	late summer
Scirpus lacustris	Common Bulrush	1-2 m.	WS - 20 cm.	late summer
S. maritimus	Sea Club Rush	1-1.75 m.	DS - 20 cm.	late summer
S. tabernaemontani zebrinus	Porcupine Quill Rush, Zebra Rush	1.4 m.	WS - 20 cm.	late summer
Sparganium erectum	Branched Bur Reed	1 m.	to 45 cm.	late summer
Trollius europaeus	Globe Flower	45 cm.	DS - WS	summer
Typha angustifolia	Lesser Reed Mace	1-2.2 m.	WS - 60 cm.	autumn
T. latifolia	Greater Reed Mace	1.5 - 2.75 cm.	WS - 60 cm.	autumn
T. Laxmanii		75 cm. - 1.2 m.	WS · 20 cm.	autumn
T. minima		30-75 cm.	WS - 10 cm.	autumn
T. Shuttleworthii		1 - 1.3 m.	WS - 30 cm.	autumn
Veronica beccabunga	Brooklime, Speedwell	20 cm.	WS - 5 cm.	late spring-autumn
Zantedeschia aethiopica *(Calla aethiopica Richardia africana)*	Arum Lily	60- 90 cm.	WS - 30 cm.	summer

Appendix III: Ferns

Asplenium trichomanes – Maidenhair Spleenwort

Thelypteris phegopteris – Beech Fern

Adiantum capillus veneris – True Maidenhair Fern

LATIN NAME	COMMON NAME	HEIGHT	HABITAT
Adiantum capillus veneris	True Maidenhair Fern	60 cm.	DS deep shade
A. pedatum	Hardy Maidenhair Fern	60 cm.	DS deep shade
Asplenium trichomanes	Maidenhair Spleenwort		Dry walls, partial shade
Athyrium filix-femina	Lady Fern	1 m.	WS partial or deep shade
Blechnum penna-marina		15 cm.	DS
B. spicant		70 cm.	DS
B. tabulare		45-90 cm.	WS
Dryopteris dilatata	Broad Prickly-toothed Buckler Fern	90 cm. - 1.8 m. versatile	
Matteuccia struthiopteris	Ostrich Feather Fern, Shuttlecock Fern	90 cm.	DS partial or deep shade
Onoclea sensibilis	Sensitive Fern	60 cm.	DS - WS or even shallow water, shade preférred
Osmunda regalis	Royal Fern	1.5 m.	WS
Phyllitis scolopendrium (Asplenium)	Hart's Tongue	45 cm.	DS - WS shade
Polypodium diversifolium		30 cm.	DS suited to walls
Polystichum setiferum	Soft Shield Fern	70 cm.	
Thelypteris phegopteris	Beech Fern	30 cm.	DS

Appendix IV: Koi Carp Definitions

Koi carp are classified according to colour and colour pattern. The range and variety is enormous and new colour patterns are continually being developed. The following represents some of the better known and more commonly used descriptive terms. Single-coloured Koi are described as:

Hi or *goi*	: red	*Kia*	: gold
Sumi	: black	*Gin*	: silver
Cha	: brown	*Beni*	: orange-red
Ki	: yellow	*Shiro*	: white

Matsuba : pine cone, a descriptive term referring to a conspicuous line or lines of scales along the flank, which are conspicuous by virtue of their colour or hue. *Hi matsuba*, for example, would be a fish with the overall colour of red and a darker line of flanking scales.

Ogon Koi are those varieties whose scales have a distinctly metallic sheen. A *gin matsuba* would be one with a silvery blue sheen, as compared with, say, a *Kia matsuba* which has the appearance of being clothed in metallic gold.

Two-colour Koi include: *Kohaku* a variety whose basic colour is white with red patterning. The mark of a good *Kohaku* is that the scales are truly white, snow white preferably, and not tinged with pink.

(Overfeeding Koi with pellets containing colour enhancers can turn white scales slightly pink.) There are innumerable forms of *Kohaku*.

Other two-colour varieties included *Shiro bekko* which is a white fish with black markings, and *Ki bekko*, yellow with black markings. A white metallic fish with silver or gold patterning goes under the name of *Hariwake*. Blue is also found among Koi carp as the *Hana Shusui*, which has red markings over a blue background, the red running along the flanks, and the scales along the back being a darker blue.

Three-coloured Koi are referred to as *Sanke* or *Sanshoku*, the principal colours usually being red, black and white. Blue sometimes makes an appearance. Four-coloured Koi are bred, and there is even *Goshiki* which is a five-coloured fish with shades of blue (light and dark), red, white and black.

Among the many patterns which have been given recognition with descriptive names is the *Tancho* fish, distinguished by having a red spot or crest on its head. The name *Tancho* derives from a bird (a crane), the *Tancho zura*, which is said to have a happy disposition, an appropriate piece of imagery for a garden inhabitant, too. Koi are notable not only for their splendid colours, but for their graceful, placid ways.

Appendix V: The International Water Lily Society

If you wish to keep in touch with developments in water gardening and exchange ideas and information with those involved in aquatic horticulture, both professionals and amateurs, there is now a society for just this purpose. The International Water Lily Society was founded in 1984 in Maryland, USA.

The Society is the official registration body for *Nymphaea*, and publishes a regular newsletter which is distributed to all members. An international symposium is held annually, at which distinguished lecturers are invited to speak on varied topics and at which garden visits are organised. As of writing, membership of the Society extends over four continents, North America, Europe, Australia and Asia.

For further information, contact:
The Secretary,
The International Water Lily Society,
PO Box 104,
Buckeystown,
MD 21717,
U.S.A.

Or

The Secretary,
The International Water Lily Society,
Wycliffe Hall Botanical Gardens,
Wycliffe Hall,
Barnard Castle,
DL12 9TS,
England.

Index

All marginal and bog plants described in Chapters 5 and 6 are listed in Appendix II, and ferns described in Chapter 6 are listed in Appendix III. Numbers in italics refer to illustrations.